YORK NOTES

General Editors: Professor A.N. Jeffares (*Univ...*
of Stirling) & Professor Suheil Bushrui (*American*
University of Beirut)

Riy...

D0723284

Henry James

THE TURN OF THE SCREW

Notes by Mary Y. Hallab

PH D (LOUISIANA) *Assistant Professor of English*
American University of Beirut

LONGMAN
YORK PRESS

YORK PRESS
Immeuble Esseily, Place Riad Solh, Beirut.

LONGMAN GROUP LIMITED
London
*Associated companies, branches and representatives
throughout the world*

© Librairie du Liban 1980

First published 1980
ISBN 0 582 78203 1

Printed in Hong Kong by
Sheck Wah Tong Printing Press Ltd

Contents

Part 1

Introduction

The life of Henry James

Henry James was born in New York City in 1843 and was the second son in a family of five children. He was named after his father, Henry James, who was well known among intellectuals of his time, mostly for his personality and some of his ideas rather than for his writing, which never achieved much success. Henry's mother was Mary Robertson Walsh, a loving woman whose husband and children were completely devoted to her. His older brother, William James, became one of America's great psychologists and philosophers.

Henry James's paternal grandfather was an Irish immigrant who had come to America and settled in New York. Through hard work and an acute business sense, he made a large fortune. In religion, he was a strict Calvinist who raised his children according to a rigid Protestantism. His son, Henry James's father, rejected this narrow Calvinism; he brought up his own children, including our author, in an atmosphere of liberalism and tolerance.

Henry James Sr. also rejected the business world of his father. Fortunately, he was able to support his family comfortably on his inheritance. Thus he was free to devote his time to his family and to propagating, unsuccessfully, his strange and visionary ideas; for he was something of a philosopher and a mystic. In general, his beliefs were rejected, or ignored, by his own sons. His intensely democratic spirit, for example, was never part of Henry James's thinking. However, his son Henry did inherit his father's good-heartedness, his tolerance, his love of life, his high-mindedness. Like his father, he believed that morality is a matter of *being* as well as *doing*; it is a natural goodness rather than a rigid adherence to a set of principles.

The James family was lively and loving. They were always together and often engaged in lively and aggressive discussion, in which the children participated. The father had many friends among literary men and thinkers in America and Europe, including Thomas Carlyle (1795–1881) and Ralph Waldo Emerson (1803–1882). James's mother was quiet and reserved, and her second son, Henry, was very much like her in this sense. In his autobiographical work written in later years, he recalls that he often felt like an outsider in his noisy and active family; for he was himself somewhat withdrawn and shy and was hindered in his speech by a slight stammer.

His father did not want to force his children to accept any rigid set of beliefs. He desired that they should have a broad experience of life and form their own opinions. Thus, their education was somewhat erratic. They were changed from school to school and from tutor to tutor; they seldom remained in one school for more than a year. In contrast to his elder brother William, Henry was a poor student, especially in science and mathematics, although he was always docile and cooperative. But he read extensively, everything he could, from Shakespeare to Hawthorne, and thus educated himself in his own way, according to his own interests.

Henry was educated, too, through visits to art exhibitions and to the theatre with his family. He loved the glitter and romance of the stage, and early in life he developed the habit, revealed in his autobiography, of thinking of people and events as actors and actions in a drama or novel. Even as a child he regarded himself as primarily an observer rather than an actor in life, and as he grew older, he devoted himself more and more to this role. Thus his life seems strangely free of incident or adventure; for example, he never married, never seems to have had a love affair, though the love affairs of others play a large role in his works.

When he was twelve years old, the family went to Europe where they remained intermittently for five years. Here, again, Henry attended numerous schools, but again he learned most from his visits to art galleries and places of cultural and historical interest.

His extensive reading, much of it in European literature, had prepared him to think of Europe as a world of excitement and romance. He was not disappointed. He never lost his love for the greatness, the tradition, the picturesqueness, the fullness of life, the culture of Europe, which he developed in his youth, and which he found lacking in the rough and business-like world of America. He later came to regard these early years in Europe as an 'initiatory' period, in which his personality and interests received their special direction. He learned to accept himself as he was; he learned to turn what seemed to be a disadvantage, his passion for quiet observation, into an advantage, a method of learning which provided the basis for his future greatness as a student and a recorder of human manners and psychology.

The family returned home at the outbreak of the American Civil War in 1861. Henry's younger brothers, Garth Wilkinson (Wilky) and Robertson, enlisted in the Northern army and were both discharged; Wilky was quite seriously wounded. Henry was prevented from enlisting by an injury to his back; the nature of this injury is not known, but it caused him much pain for many years. Following his brother William, Henry took up the study of art for a short time. But he soon recognised his lack of talent and gave it up completely. He was already thinking seriously of becoming a writer. He did enroll briefly in the Harvard University Law School, but spent most of his time writing. In 1864, he published his first tales in American journals: 'A Tragedy of Error', which was unsigned, and 'The Story of a Year'. These stories were quickly followed by others, as well as by articles and reviews. From this time on, Henry James devoted his entire life to his chosen work.

In 1869, he again travelled to Europe, this time alone, for a stay of fourteen months. During this trip, he received the news of the death, at the age of twenty-four, of his adored cousin Mary Temple. Some writers believe that James was secretly in love with her and that her death led to his failure to marry. In any case, he felt deep sorrow at the loss of her lively and vivacious personality. She provided the model for several of the heroines of his novels.

He was again in Europe from 1872 to 1874. He took rooms for some time in Italy, where he began work on *Roderick Hudson*, his first novel. It deals with one of the most common of his themes—that of the American confronting the rich culture and the corruption of Europe. By this time, he was well started on his literary career; the cost of this trip was financed in part by a series of travel writings which he sent home for publication in an American journal.

These two trips decided James's future for him: as a writer, he was happier and more comfortable in Europe, and he decided to make his residence there. Perhaps, to fulfil himself as a freely creative individual, James needed to live apart from the almost smothering affection and sometimes aggressive criticism of his family, among whom he had always played a quiet and inferior role.

In 1875, at the age of thirty-two, James settled in Paris. There, he became friendly with some members of that important literary circle which included such writers as Gustave Flaubert, Guy de Maupassant, Emile Zola, Alphonse Daudet, and Ivan Turgenev, with whom he became quite close. But on the whole, he found the French writers provincial and devoted to a new kind of 'realism' in their work which did not suit his taste.

In 1876, he moved to London; he lived in or near London for the rest of his life, except for numerous visits to the Continent and, of course, to America. It was during these years that he began to deal fully with the 'international theme' in his novels and tales, the theme of the problems and conflicts of Americans and Europeans, the New World and the Old, confronting each other's cultures.

For the sake of convenience, James's life and writing are usually divided into three major periods; the first period begins with his early literary efforts and ends with the publication of his long novel, *The Portrait of a Lady* in 1880. Some best known works of this period are those dealing with the international subject, *Roderick Hudson, The*

American, The Europeans. One work of this period, *Daisy Miller*, published in 1879, was a great success and brought him his first popular recognition as a writer. It is a tale of a young, free-spirited but naïve American girl caught up in and destroyed by the rigid, conventional and corrupt old culture of Europe. Its theme of an innocent young lady threatened by evil which, because of her inexperience, she cannot fully comprehend, is pervasive in James's works and appears later in *The Turn of the Screw*.

In London, James was welcomed as the brilliant and promising author of *Daisy Miller*, and he quickly became part of the social and literary life. He became acquainted with such prominent literary figures as Alfred Tennyson, Andrew Lang, Robert Browning, Walter Pater, George Meredith and Matthew Arnold. Yet, in spite of a very active social schedule, he kept up a full programme of writing.

In 1881 he returned to America for a visit. While he was there, in 1882, his mother died. Seemingly unable to live without her, his father died in the same year, followed by his younger brother Wilky. On the death of his parents, Henry came into a small inheritance, which he turned over to his invalid sister Alice. He was now able to make his own way, modestly, on the revenues from his writings.

The second period of his writing career was marked by a wide variety of literary experiments. In the first place, determined to write a truly great novel, James produced *The Bostonians*, *The Princess Casamassima* and *The Tragic Muse*. These works have characteristics of the naturalistic novel in that they are full of realistic detail, are concerned with social problems, and stress the influence of environment on character. But public indifference to these works, coupled with his deep personal losses, called up in James the feeling of failure and uncertainty which plagued him throughout his life, and deepened his desire for recognition.

This desire for popular success led him to turn to the theatre, for which, in his lifetime, he wrote several plays, none of which were really successful. His brief career as a playwright came to a sudden and tragic halt with the embarrassing public failure of his play *Guy Domville* in 1894. According to his biographers, the time following the failure of his play was a period of great despair in his life. Yet, with his usual courage, he forced himself to continue with his work.

His stories of this second period include a number of tales which might have been about the author himself. In some the hero is an artist who has failed or is misunderstood. In others, the hero is a man who comes to regret too late in life that he has not led a full life. Also, in this period, James wrote a number of stories about children or young people who are neglected or abused by frightening and overpowering adults who make use of them for their own wicked purposes, such as *What Maisie Knew* and *The Turn of the Screw*. This period also includes a number of tales of the supernatural. Many critics think that in these stories James expressed his own worries and preoccupations as a writer, his fear of failure, his sense of being misunderstood. In his tales of ghosts and abused children, he dramatised his view of life in a letter to a friend: 'I have the imagination of disaster and see life as ferocious and sinister.'

In 1898, James moved from London to an eighteenth-century house in Rye, Sussex; this was his permanent residence for most of the rest of his life, though he kept rooms in London and made frequent use of them. (Note that this is the year he published *The Turn of the Screw*, also set in an old house named 'Bly'.) He continued to keep up his social contacts; among his many visitors were his neighbours, H.G. Wells, Ford Maddox Ford, Joseph Conrad, and Stephen Crane, as well as his brother William and the author, Edith Wharton, from America.

The final period of his career, beginning around 1900, is marked by the publication, between 1900 and 1904, of three of his greatest works, *The Ambassadors*, *The Wings of the Dove*, and *The Golden Bowl*. In these long and difficult novels he returned to the international subject of his earlier period, but on a grander and more magnificent scale, with a far greater subtlety and intricacy. The novels show the gradual change in James's prose style over the years, from one that was clear and direct, to the rich, full, subtle, but extremely difficult style of his later period, by means of which he attempted to represent the complex conscious-ness of his characters, their various levels of awareness, their intense but sensitive reactions to experience.

In 1904, he again travelled to America, to renew old acquaintances. As a result of this trip, in 1907, the first volume of the famous New York Edition of his works appeared. James acted as editor; he selected and grouped the novels and tales to be included, and revised them carefully. For each of the twenty-four volumes (two more were added later), he wrote a preface in which he dealt with problems of composition and expressed his convictions as to the nature and function of literature.

By this time, he was a prominent public figure, noted for the wit and weight of his conversation and respected by discerning critics for the unequalled quality of his writing, his mastery of the technique of prose fiction which distinguish his works as the high point in the history of the English novel. In 1911, he received an honorary degree from Harvard University in America, and in 1912, from the University of Oxford. Shortly before his death in 1916, he received the Order of Merit from the British government. In 1913, on his seventieth birthday, he was honoured by over two hundred and fifty of his friends, who presented him with a golden bowl and commissioned a portrait of him to be done by his friend, the famous painter John Singer Sargent.

In 1892, after years spent in England as an invalid, his sister Alice died. In 1910, his brothers William and Robertson died. James alone survived from his immediate family, but still maintained, as had his dying heroine in *The Wings of the Dove*, the necessity of striving on, of devoting himself to living fully until the end. Probably as a release for his sorrows, he began the autobiographical volumes that deal with his boyhood and early youth, *A Small Boy and Others* and *Notes of a Son and Brother*; a third volume, *The Middle Years* was left unfinished.

In 1914, war broke out between England and Germany. James threw himself into the war effort with surprising energy. Some believe that he was unconsciously making up for his failure as a young man to go to battle in the American Civil War. In any case he was deeply loyal to his adopted home, England, and was embarrassed that America, at that point, had refused to come to the aid of the Allies. To demonstrate his loyalty, in 1915, he renounced his American citizenship and became a British subject.

He died on 28 February 1916, as a result of a stroke. His body was cremated, and, as he had requested, the ashes were returned to be buried in the family plot in a cemetery in Cambridge, Massachusetts.

James's reputation as a writer

Henry James is now considered to be one of America's great novelists. But during his lifetime he was little appreciated by the general public, though he was the centre of a small but devoted group of followers who recognised his great genius. After his death his reputation dropped even lower; for some time his works were virtually neglected by critics and readers. This neglect was partly the result of a change in literary taste. The years after the First World War were a time of rapid social change, of the rise of industrialisation, of socialism and the motor car. The reading public no longer had the time or patience for the slow and intricate Jamesian sentences, the leisurely pace of his works, usually centred on a single action around which the characters move in stately grandeur. Furthermore, the public now preferred novels full of realistic and concrete detail; they demanded a greater focus on the lower classes (which were almost completely neglected in James's works), with an emphasis on the determining effect of environment on character. But James's novels are set almost entirely in the upper middle class or aristocratic world of Europe and America; thus they were regarded as too genteel, even snobbish, remote from and irrelevant to the great social problems facing a new era. His characters were frequently criticised as being mere minds, without bodies, without substance, floating aimlessly in a dream world of wealth and privilege, and therefore without real problems or interest. Moreover, in America, James's reputation suffered from the opinion that he had betrayed his true self by leaving his country and dealing primarily with Europe.

Yet, today, James is considered by many to be one of the great realistic novelists, not because of his few attempts at realism in his middle period, but because of the psychological realism of his works; he is often thought of as the father of the modern psychological novel. For in his novels and his tales James dealt with human relationships, with, as he said, 'the very atmosphere of the mind' of his characters as they subtly recorded and responded to the minds and actions of others. He was especially concerned with the problems, not of environmental determinism, but of free moral choice; his tales almost always focus on a single problem or action concerning which a choice, a decision, must be made. This choice will determine the destiny of the person who makes it. Very often this fateful decision must be made within an ambiguous, an unclear, and complex context, and its results will not be clear until it is too late to repair them.

The Turn of the Screw

The Turn of the Screw is a novelette, that is, a short novel, a genre, or literary type, in which James excelled. It focuses on a few characters and one action which occurs over a relatively short time period, five months, to be exact. It has neither the realism, the breadth, nor the complexity of the novel, though like the novel and in spite of the supernatural element, it has the 'air of reality' James considered essential to fiction. The action builds gradually towards one climax, one high point, which quickly comes to a *dénouement*, a resolution or conclusion.

'The Turn of the Screw' as a Gothic romance

In creating this tale, James drew on a number of popular story types. It is, first, a ghost story, a tale of supernatural terror, and as such it makes use of many of the devices of the Gothic novel. The Gothic novel was a tale of terror belonging to the genre, or literary type, of the romance. In general the prose romance is distinguished from the novel by an air of unreality, a remote, exotic or unreal setting in which anything might happen, and an attempt to arouse intense feeling in the reader. It is more ambiguous than the novel, with less realism, less concrete detail. According to James himself, in the preface to *The American* in the New York Edition, an element which characterises the romance is 'the facing of danger'. The romance, he says, deals with an intense experience in a setting isolated from the conditions of everyday life. Yet, he adds, the reader must not be fully aware of this isolation, this unrelatedness to common life, but must be made to retain the illusion of reality. Moreover, as opposed to the novel, the romance deals, James says, with those things we can never fully know, that we can never be sure of, but which we can deal with only through the circlings and uncertainties of 'our thought and our desire'.

The Turn of the Screw shares many characteristics of the Gothic romance. First, it has an element of the supernatural; it is set in an isolated place, an old house, having a dramatic or violent history which comes alive again in the present. The theme, moreover, concerns innocence threatened by a terrible evil, embodied in extraordinarily devilish characters who are ghosts. The tale is pervaded by an air of the mysterious and of horror and terror, derived from a deliberate ambiguity, a lack of clarity, not as to what will happen, but as to what *is* happening –that is, the characters find themselves entangled in a series of occurrences which cannot be explained according to reason or ordinary standards of common sense. Finally, as in the Gothic romance, there is a strong undercurrent, a suggestion of sexuality and sadism, as well as a strange and nightmare-like quality.

James showed an interest in the ghost story throughout his life. His first ghost story, published in 1868, was *A Romance of Certain Old Clothes*, about a woman who returns after death to take a grisly revenge for a wrong done to her. It shows clearly the influence of Nathaniel Hawthorne, another American writer whose work has a 'Gothic' element. James's ghost stories, then, reflect the influence of contemporary writers and the immense popularity of the Gothic romance in the nineteenth century.

Moreover, the ghost stories reflect the increasing interest, even among the highly educated, in spirits, in communication with the dead, that rose toward the end of the nineteenth century. James's brother William, was, in fact, one of the founders and president for a time of the Society for Psychical Research, an organisation seriously devoted to investigating reports of the appearances of ghosts and other 'psychical', or mental, phenomena, such as mind-reading. James was certainly aware of their activities and familiar with their reports. In fact, in his preface to *The Turn of the Screw*, he is careful to point out that his ghosts are not like those described in the records of the Society for Psychical Research, but are more like those of fairy tales—goblins, elves, imps, demons. For while the commonly reported ghosts usually appear for no particular reason to persons unknown to them, *his* ghosts have a purpose, an intention, as do the fairies, elves, demons, of folklore.

'The Turn of the Screw' as a folktale

Thus, in addition to the Gothic romance, James drew a good deal on popular folklore for this tale; for its motif, that of children bewitched, enchanted, or threatened by creatures from another world—or by the dead—is a well-known folklore theme. In his preface to the tale in the

New York Edition, James calls it a 'fairy tale pure and simple'. And it is from the simplicity and the power of this universally popular story pattern that the tale draws its fascination.

'The Turn of the Screw' as a psychological study

Finally, the tale anticipates the modern psychological novel in that it deals not so much with ghosts but with their effects on those who see them. In many of James's tales of the supernatural, the ghosts, not necessarily evil, represent the *past*, personal or ancestral, of the person who sees them, as in *Owen Wingrave* and *The Sense of the Past*. In others, the ghost is even more clearly 'psychological' in that it represents some aspect of the person who sees it, as in *The Jolly Corner*, in which the ghost is the 'double', the other self, of its viewer. Thus the ghosts have a psychological relationship with those they haunt and usually influence their lives in some way.

It is in all these senses that we must read *The Turn of the Screw*: as a tale of terror, as a modern elaboration of a popular folklore theme, and as a study in human psychology.

The writing of 'The Turn of the Screw'

Like many of James's novels and tales, *The Turn of the Screw* is based on an anecdote, a little story, told him by a friend. In an entry in his notebooks of 12 January 1895, he refers to a 'ghost-story' told him 'before the fire' by E.A. Benson, the Archbishop of Canterbury, who had heard it from a friend, a young lady. The story was about orphaned children left in the care of wicked and depraved servants, who corrupt the children. The servants die and return to haunt the children to entice them to their death. James says of this anecdote, '. . . there is a suggestion of a strangely gruesome effect in it. The story to be told . . . by an outside spectator, observer.' He did not get around to writing the tale until two years later, in the autumn of 1897. Yet the circumstances of the telling of the original anecdote, as well as its general outline, are preserved in James's version of it. Notice, too, James's desire to achieve *effect*; for it is not in the original anecdote but in his retelling of it that the effect is achieved—an effect of horror appropriate to the Gothic romance.

A note on the text

The Turn of the Screw was first published in serial form, that is, in parts, in the journal, *Collier's Weekly*, volume 20, number 17 (27 January 1898) to volume 21, number 2 (16 April 1898). It was immediately republished in two separate collections of James's tales; *The Two Magics: The Turn of the Screw and Covering End*, in England, by William Heinemann in October 1898; and in America, in *The Two Magics*, by the Macmillan Company, also in October 1898. It was reprinted as one of the four tales included in volume 12 of the New York Edition of James's works, published in New York by Charles Scribner's Sons and in London by Macmillan and Company in 1908. As with most of the tales published in the New York Edition, James made a number of revisions in wording, but in the case of *The Turn of the Screw*, he made no major changes in the text. The preface to this edition contains an interesting discussion of the tale, to which we shall refer later.

During James's life, *The Turn of the Screw* was also reprinted as the first volume of *The Uniform Tales of Henry James*, published by Martin Secker in London, April 1915. This publication retains the revisions made in the New York Edition.

No original manuscript for the story remains in existence.

The Turn of the Screw has been one of the most popular and most frequently reprinted of James's tales. It can be found today in any number of paperback editions, where it is usually included with other tales by James. For example, it is available in the Penguin Modern Classics series, where it is reprinted along with two other tales by James, *The Pupil* and *The Third Person*.

The present popularity of the tale is evident not only in the many modern issues of it, but in the fact that it has been made into an opera, with music by Benjamın Britten and libretto by Myfanwy Piper (1954), a successful Broadway play entitled *The Innocents* (1950), and an excellent movie of the same name, starring Deborah Kerr (1961).

Part 2

Summaries
of THE TURN OF THE SCREW

A general summary

The tale is begun by a narrator whose name is never given. He and some friends are sitting around a fire in an old country house one Christmas Eve. They are telling ghost stories. Another member of the group, Douglas, promises them a truly horrifying tale; it is written on a manuscript which he must send home for. But the next night he gives a brief introduction to it. The writer of the manuscript was a young woman who had once been a governess to his sister. She gave him the manuscript before she died. The others guess that Douglas was in love with the governess.

She was the daughter of a poor country parson who went to London in answer to an advertisement for a governess. She was interviewed by a handsome and charming gentleman; she immediately fell in love with him. He employed her to go to his country house at Bly to care for his orphaned niece, Flora, and her brother Miles. Miles was away at school but he would be home for the summer. Her employer set one condition to the work: she was never to bother him, but to handle everything herself.

The rest of the tale is a copy of the governess's manuscript. It was made by the unnamed narrator from the original.

The governess arrives at Bly one June afternoon. It is a large old country house set in beautiful surroundings. The little girl, Flora, is beautiful and charming; and Mrs Grose, the housekeeper, is a plain, decent, simple woman, who is obviously glad to see her.

Before Miles arrives, the governess is distressed to receive a letter from school saying that he has been dismissed because he is harmful to the others. She and Mrs Grose decide not to inform the children's uncle of the letter. Mrs Grose insists that Miles is as good as his sister, and when he arrives the governess agrees. The summer days pass pleasantly; she gives lessons to the children, and thinks about how she will please their uncle with her good work.

One day, while daydreaming about her employer, she sees a man on one of the towers of the old house and wonders who he might be, but does not mention him to anyone. Later, alone in the house, she again sees the same man peering in at a window. She feels sure he has come for the children. She describes him to Mrs Grose, who identifies him as

Peter Quint, the master's former valet. He was a wicked man who had been in charge of the children. But he had died mysteriously. The governess begins to think that she has been called to perform a heroic duty—to protect these innocent children.

One afternoon, sitting with Flora by a small lake, she sees a woman in black. Though Flora appears not to notice, the governess is sure that she too sees the figure. This woman is later identified by Mrs Grose as the former governess, Miss Jessel, who is also dead. According to Mrs Grose, Miss Jessel had been carrying on a romance with the evil and low Peter Quint.

The governess begins to suspect that the ghosts communicate with the children. She finds out from Mrs Grose that the children had been much under their influence while they were alive. But her suspicions are allayed because of the perfect goodness, charm, and intelligence of the children.

Before dawn, one morning, she again sees the ghost of Quint on the stairs. But he disappears as she boldly stares at him. Returning to her room, she finds Flora gazing out of the window. She does not believe that Flora was simply looking for her. For nights she searches the house for the ghosts, but only once sees Miss Jessel sitting sadly on the steps.

Eleven nights after seeing Quint on the stairs, she wakes to find Flora again staring out of the window. Going into a nearby room in the tower, she sees Miles outside on the grass staring up at something above her. Later, Miles tells her that he and Flora were playing a trick on her but she does not believe him. She comes increasingly to think that the children are cooperating in the ghosts' efforts to entice them to evil and destruction, that all their goodness is a pretence. Yet she refuses to notify their uncle for fear of his anger.

Autumn comes with no new sign of the ghosts. Fearful of damaging her relationship with the children, the governess never mentions the ghosts to them; but she often senses that the ghosts are present and feels that the children are under their influence. The children begin to ask about their uncle; they want him to come to Bly. They write him letters, but the governess never mails them.

One Sunday, on the way to church, Miles tells her he wants to go to school again, and threatens to inform his uncle if she does not help him. Agitated, she decides to run away and returns alone to the house. Entering the schoolroom, she sees Miss Jessel seated at the desk. She cries out and the ghost vanishes. She finally decides she must write to the children's uncle.

That evening she has a long talk with Miles in which she tries to get him to confess why he was dismissed from school, but she learns nothing except that he wishes to be left alone. Passionately, she tells him she would do anything to help him. He shrieks. A gust of cold air blows out the candle, although the windows are closed.

The next day she has written the letter. After dinner Miles plays the piano for her, and she falls into a daydream. Suddenly she notices that Flora is gone; the children have again tricked her in order to allow Flora to get away to see Miss Jessel. While she and Mrs Grose rush out to find Flora, Miles will receive Peter Quint. Before going, she puts the letter on the hall table to be taken to town.

They find Flora alone by the lake, smiling innocently. For the first time, the governess asks Flora about Miss Jessel. Then, across the lake, she sees Miss Jessel and cries out. But Mrs Grose cannot see the ghost. Flora screams that she too sees nothing and demands that Mrs Grose take her away, which she does. The governess realises that Flora is lying, but she can do nothing. That night, Flora sleeps with Mrs Grose. The governess never sees her again.

The next day, Mrs Grose tells her that Flora has been ill all night and says shocking things about the governess—using bad language she must have learned from Quint. The governess feels justified in her suspicions and relieved that Mrs Grose now believes her story. She tells Mrs Grose to take Flora to town that day and leave Miles at Bly with her. He may confess, and if he does so, he is 'saved', and so is she. She recollects the letter and is distressed when Mrs Grose tells her that Miles must have taken it.

Flora and Mrs Grose leave; the governess does not see Miles until dinner. After dinner, she asks him if he has taken the letter. As she does so Quint appears at the window, but she realises that Miles is unaware of his presence. She is overjoyed when Miles confesses that he did take the letter and read it. At the same time, the ghost vanishes.

Under pressure, Miles admits that at school he 'said things' that must have been bad. The governess has a brief but frightening thought that perhaps he is innocent, but she continues to urge him to tell her everything. To her dismay, Quint again appears at the window. Miles is aware that something is wrong, but he can see nothing. She wants him to name the ghost; and, trying to comply, he asks if it is Miss Jessel. Then realising his mistake, he cries out, 'Peter Quint—you devil!' The ghost disappears, but the strain has been too much; Miles dies in her arms.

Detailed summaries

The Prologue

The tale begins with a prologue, an introductory section, in which we learn something of its background and how it came to be told.

A group of friends are spending the Christmas holidays together in an old house. One of them, whose name is never given to us, actually tells the whole story; he is the narrator.

The friends are sitting around the fire on Christmas Eve listening to ghost stories. A man named Griffin has just told them a tale about a ghost that appeared to a little boy and his mother. Another member of the party, Douglas, says that he can tell an even more gruesome tale about two children, which, he says, will give 'the effect another turn of the screw'.

The story is written down on an old manuscript which he must send for. The manuscript was written by the woman to whom the events occurred. She has been dead for twenty years, but before she died, she sent the manuscript to Douglas. His friends guess that Douglas was in love with her; but he denies it, for she was ten years older than he. She was governess to his younger sister. She was, he says, one of 'the most agreeable' women he has ever known. She told him the story one summer afternoon, when he was on vacation from his studies at the university. The narrator guesses that the governess—whose name is never given to us—was also in love, and Douglas agrees. Douglas leaves the room, and we learn that he has been silent about the story for forty years.

The second night, Christmas night, Douglas tells them more about the governess; she was the youngest daughter of a poor country parson in Hampshire, a rural county south-west of London. At the age of twenty, needing work, she went to London in answer to an advertisement. There, she met her future employer; he was 'a gentleman, a bachelor in the prime of life', and he appeared to the simple girl to be as handsome and romantic as a hero in a novel.

He asked her to go to Bly, his country home in Essex, a county in south-east England, to serve as governess to his niece, Flora, and during school holidays, to his nephew, Miles. They were the children of his dead brother, for whom he was now guardian. They lived at Bly under the care of the housekeeper, Mrs Grose; she was in charge, but 'below stairs only'. The previous governess had died. There were other servants in the house, but the governess would be in complete control.

Nervous and fearful of being lonely at Bly, the governess waited two days before accepting the job. Yet, in her two meetings with him, she developed a great passion for her employer. However, at their second meeting, he insisted on one condition: that she should take care of all problems herself and never bother him about the children. Overcome by his charm, she agreed to this condition. She never saw him again.

After this introduction, Douglas stops until the next evening, the third night, a Thursday, when he opens the manuscript and begins to read.

COMMENTARY: This introductory section sets the story in a frame; that is, we are not told the story directly, but we hear it as it was told to others. In fact, the story is told by *three* storytellers, or narrators: (i) the governess tells it to Douglas (when he is about twenty years old), and twenty years later, she gives him a notebook in which she has written it down; (*ii*) after keeping silent for forty years, Douglas tells the story to friends and later gives the manuscript to one of them; (*iii*) this friend, never named, tells the story to us, first, in the Prologue, as he heard it from Douglas, and later, beginning with Chapter One, as the governess wrote it down.

In the Prologue, we are introduced to the story as it is told, at night, around a fire, when ghost stories are particularly believable. Thus the Prologue sets up a mood, a feeling of mystery, which will allow the reader to accept the strange events he will read of later. This air of mystery is further strengthened by the narrator's refusal to be specific and clear about what actually happens—a tendency we will see more of later as the tale progresses. For example, we are given relatively little information about the governess, not even her name. Douglas's feelings for her are suggested, never clearly stated. In fact, after this introduction, Douglas disappears from the story, as does the narrator; from now on, we hear the tale as the governess recorded it.

We should notice the reference to the title in the second paragraph of the tale. According to the narrator, the addition of a second child adds two turns to the screw, that is, another 'twist' to the story. As we read, we will find many such 'turns'; for example, there is already a 'twist' in the fact that Douglas loves the governess, who is too old for him, while the governess loves or has loved the children's uncle, who is above her in social class. Other such 'turns' in the story represent changes in the direction of the story from what we have been led to expect. Thus, the title, *The Turn of the Screw*, suggests the way the story will develop by twists and turns, as a screw progresses through a piece of wood. Moreover, the title suggests the medieval device of torture, the 'thumbscrew', in which the victim's thumbs were squeezed slowly with a screw, usually to force him to confess. As the story progresses, this suggestion will take on further meaning, though here the 'torture' is mental rather than physical.

NOTES AND GLOSSARY

visitation: a visit to someone by a ghost or spirit of the dead

apparition: a ghost or spirit which appears to a living person

interlocutor: a person taking part in a conversation

uncanny: mysterious, strange, unnatural

He had broken a thickness of ice, the formation of many a winter . . .: this is an analogy, a kind of comparison, which shows how difficult it has been for Douglas to speak about this matter after many years of silence (the 'thickness of ice')

scruples:	doubts as to what is right and wrong
Raison de plus:	(*French*) even the more reason
manuscript:	a handwritten book or document
governess:	a person who supervises and directs the education of children, usually in their home
reticence:	a tendency to be silent and reserved
'candle-stuck':	put candles in their holders
auditory:	a group of listeners, an audience
parson:	a clergyman, a man of the Church
trepidation:	agitation, anxiety, alarm
patron:	a person who supports another, who acts as helper and protector
a gentleman:	a member of the upper classes; also, a man who has good manners
in the prime of life:	in the period of greatest perfection and vigour
vicarage:	the house of a vicar, a clergyman; the house in which the governess grew up
the spoils of travel and the trophies of the chase:	the objects brought back from travels and the objects which give evidence of success in hunting
guardian:	a person placed by law to be in charge of the affairs of another, usually a child
below stairs only:	with the servants, who usually lived and worked in the lower levels of the house; Mrs Grose's position is not so high as that of a governess who lived and worked with the family 'above stairs'.
solicitor:	a lawyer who is paid to handle another's business and legal affairs

Chapter One

(Beginning with this chapter, through to the end of the book, the story is told in the words of the governess as she wrote them in her manuscript.)

Late one June afternoon, the governess arrives at Bly. The house is a large and fine country home, set in a beautiful lawn. At the door are Mrs Grose, the housekeeper, and the little girl, Flora, who is the most beautiful child the governess has ever seen.

That night, the governess is able to sleep only a little. She is excited and impressed with the magnificence of the house. She had worried about her relationship with Mrs Grose, and is relieved to find that she is a plain, simple, sensible woman, who seems very happy to see her.

Early the next morning, she thinks she hears the cry of a child and a light footstep outside her door; later these sounds will have more meaning to her. She is delighted with the idea of helping to form little Flora, who is sweet and calm. Mrs Grose tells her that she will also love Miles, who will arrive from school on Friday. The governess confesses to Mrs Grose that she had been fascinated with the children's uncle. Mrs Grose replies that many others have also found him attractive.

The next day, she explores the house and grounds with Flora. Flora confidently shows her the many rooms, the long halls, the crooked staircases, and even an 'old machicolated square tower'. She imagines she is in a 'castle of romance', and that Flora is a 'rosy sprite'; living here will be like living in a fairy tale. She thinks of the house as a huge, drifting ship with herself at the helm.

COMMENTARY: In this chapter we meet two of the major characters and learn something about them, as they appear to the governess. Mrs Grose's character will remain much the same throughout the story, but Flora's will appear to change as the story progresses.

We also learn about the governess. She is quite imaginative and tends to dramatise herself and her situation, that is, to see herself as a character in a story and to imagine her situation as more exciting and interesting than, perhaps, it really is. Her final thought about herself as captain of a ship suggests her concern about her responsibilities as well as her sense of self-importance.

NOTES AND GLOSSARY:

succession of flights and drops: a series of ups and downs; the governess's feelings are sometimes happy and optimistic, sometimes worried and pessimistic

see-saw: back and forth or up and down movement, characteristic of the governess's feelings throughout the tale

throbs: strong beats or pulsations, like heartbeats

a commodious fly: a light, public carriage for passengers, here, a comfortable one

rooks: black crows, large black birds

liberality: generosity

figured draperies: curtains with designs on them

as so many things thrown in: as so many extra good things added

brooded: thought about long and deeply

starting: moving suddenly, as in surprise

fancies: ideas with little foundation, hallucinations

one of Raphael's holy infants: Raphael (1483–1520) was a painter of the Italian Renaissance whose works include pictures of Mary and the baby Jesus, whose faces reveal deep, inner peacefulness

prodigious: extraordinary in force, size or strength
gratified looks: looks that are understood and responded to
roundabout allusions: indirect references
carried away: influenced beyond reason; the governess is frequently 'carried away' by her feelings for the
children and for their uncle
agitation: a disturbed and nervous condition
machicolated: having a projecting gallery with open spaces,
through which, as on a castle tower, weapons might
be used against an enemy
sprite: a fairy or an elf; a supernatural being, usually very
small, with magical powers
at the helm: at the wheel by which a ship is steered

Chapter Two

The second evening, the governess receives a letter, sent from Miles's
school to his uncle, who has not bothered to open it. It contains the distressing news that Miles has been dismissed from school because he is
harmful to the other students. Mrs Grose finds the whole idea ridiculous,
for she believes that Miles is as good and charming as his sister; and,
besides, he is only ten years old.

The next day, the governess learns from Mrs Grose about her pre-
decessor, the former governess, who was, like her, young and pretty. In
the conversation, Mrs Grose refers to some man, other than the
children's uncle, who liked pretty women, but she immediately covers
up her reference. She does reveal that the former governess had gone
for a short holiday and that later she had died without ever returning to
Bly.

COMMENTARY: The element of mystery is gradually introduced into the
story, as we are presented with some unanswered questions in Chapters
One and Two. What are the noises the governess hears on her first morning at Bly? Why was Miles dismissed from school? Who is the man that
Mrs Grose accidentally refers to and then tries to cover up? (This question will be answered, and soon.) And finally, how did the first governess
die? The young governess is left with these mysteries on which her lively
imagination quickly begins to work.

NOTES AND GLOSSARY:
disconcerted: confused, upset
wind up: finish, conclude, come to an end
attenuated: weakened or reduced in force
forebore: held back

atonement:	amends, satisfaction for a wrong done
colleague:	a person one works with; here, Mrs Grose
ambiguous:	unclear in meaning; having two or more possible meanings

Chapter Three

Miles arrives, and the governess finds him to be beautiful, innocent and charming. She is convinced that the letter from school is a mistake. But in order not to disturb his uncle, she and Mrs Grose decide not to write to him about it.

She begins giving lessons to the children. Her first impressions are confirmed: they are no trouble at all but are healthy, happy and good. She thinks of them as little grandees, royal children, who must be carefully protected. The summer days pass peacefully and quietly. The governess feels justified in having taken the job. She begins to think of herself as a remarkable person, and she hopes that the master, her employer, will someday discover this and approve of her.

One afternoon late in June, she is strolling alone in the garden and thinking of the children's uncle. She happens to look up at one of the two square towers on each side of the house. There, she sees—she believes—the children's uncle standing on its top. But she is shocked to realise that the man looking down at her is not her employer; he is someone unknown. But she sees him quite distinctly, realises that he feels quite at home. He is too far away to speak to, but he watches her intently for some time; then he slowly turns away.

COMMENTARY: Significant events occur in this chapter. First, Miles arrives, and the governess finds him as beautiful and dear as his sister. This only intensifies her wonder—and ours—about the reason for his dismissal from school. The second event is the appearance of the figure on the tower, of whom we shall learn more later. It is significant that the figure appears while the governess is daydreaming about her employer, and that she first takes him for the master. This incident is the first of the truly significant events in the mystery, and it brings to the reader's mind the first major point of suspense: who is the intruder? For James begins to build up suspense in his story by gradually presenting his main character, the governess—and the reader—with a series of strange and unexplained occurrences, which, however, at this point in the story, are not so strange that they cannot have some reasonable explanation.

NOTES AND GLOSSARY:

under an interdict: under a prohibition or a decree forbidding a person from doing something; Miles is forbidden to return to school

'It doesn't live an instant.': it has no validity, even for a short time; it does not hold up

under a charm: under the influence of magic power or enchantment

grandees: Spanish gentlemen of very high rank

take a turn: take a walk around

plump: directly

incongruous: seemingly out of place or inappropriate

crenelated: with square indentations or notches, as are often seen on the tops of castle walls

gingerbread antiquity: refers to an architectural style popular in the early part of the nineteenth century; showy and fanciful designs on buildings which were supposed to imitate the architecture of the Middle Ages.

battlements: crenelated walls

privately bred: raised and educated at home

Chapter Four

After seeing the man on the tower, the governess wonders if there is some strange secret at Bly like those she has read about in novels. She decides not to mention the man to Mrs Grose. After a period of worry, she finally concludes that he was simply a curious intruder. She again comes under the spell of the children, whom she still regards as angels, and she begins to think that the school masters who dismissed Miles were envious and vindictive.

One Sunday afternoon, preparing for church, she goes to get a pair of gloves she has left in the dining room. She is surprised to see at the window the same man she saw on the tower. Though he fixes her intently with his eyes, she realises he has not come for her. She runs outside and around to the window, but he has disappeared. She looks in through the window and startles Mrs Grose, who has followed her into the dining room.

COMMENTARY: After the first appearance of the figure on the tower, the governess immediately allows her imagination to go to work; she thinks of the strange occurrence in terms of stories she has read. Although she is very nervous, she feels that it is her duty to protect the others from worrying.

Again we are left in suspense with the question: Who is the man and what does he want?

NOTES AND GLOSSARY:

pull me up: stop me suddenly

practised upon: plotted or conspired against; the governess thinks the servants might have played a joke on her.

a mystery of Udolpho: the governess thinks of a novel, *The Mysteries of Udolpho* (1794), by Ann Radcliffe (1764–1823). It was one of the most popular of the Gothic romances; in it, the ghostly sounds and shadows which frighten the inhabitants of the castle at Udolpho turn out to be the result of natural causes, a group of robbers hiding in a castle vault

an insane, an unmentionable relative kept in unsuspected confinement: this refers to the well-known novel by Charlotte Brontë (1816–1855), *Jane Eyre*, published in 1847. In it a young woman goes to serve as a governess in a house in which strange things happen and a strange figure appears now and then. Finally, all is explained as the result of natural causes: the figure is the employer's insane wife. On her eventual death, he marries the governess, Jane Eyre. Thus, the governess of *The Turn of the Screw* thinks that the figure she sees can easily be explained. Notice that *Jane Eyre* deals with a governess's marriage to her employer, who at first seems far above her in social class; the governess's allusion to it may express her own hopes

the sisterhood: other governesses

vindictive: tending to revenge

muff: a failure

cherubs of the anecdote who had . . . nothing to whack: the governess refers to a story about little angels who are insubstantial, without bodies, and therefore cannot be physically punished

under the spell: under the influence of magic or enchantment

scrappy: in pieces, disconnected

vibration of duty and courage: the governess trembles with her sense of her duty and courage

---

Chapter Five

The governess confronts Mrs Grose, who comes out of the house to meet her. Now she tells Mrs Grose about the strange visitor. He is, she says, not a gentleman, but is low and horrible, and is a danger to the children. She describes him to Mrs Grose: he has curly red hair, a long, pale, but handsome face, with queer, red whiskers. His eyebrows are dark and arched, and his eyes are strange. He has a wide mouth with thin lips. He is smartly dressed, but in clothes that belong to someone else.

On hearing this, Mrs Grose turns white. The man is Peter Quint, the master's former valet, his personal servant; he sometimes wore the master's waistcoats. He and the former governess were at Bly, Mrs Grose says, last year. But Quint, she continues, is dead.

COMMENTARY: This chapter provides the first strange 'twist' or 'turn of the screw' of horror in the story. The governess learns that the strange visitor is a ghost and that his presence cannot be explained as due to natural causes.

The governess mentions that Quint is not a 'gentleman'. In the class structure of nineteenth-century England, 'gentlemen' were regarded as having qualities of refinement, associated with being of good family, of whom certain standards of character and behaviour were expected. The reference suggests Quint's moral 'lowness' which the governess immediately senses. This lowness is emphasised in his appearance, which reminds us of traditional pictures of the devil.

NOTES AND GLOSSARY:

my need to respect the bloom of Mrs Grose's [innocence] had dropped, without a rustle, from my shoulders . . .: a metaphor—a comparison of two unlike things; the governess means that she immediately and without thinking, as if taking off a cape, dropped her feeling that she must respect Mrs Grose's almost childlike innocence

she knew too well her place: Mrs Grose has a lower place on the social scale than the governess and must therefore support her; observe the frequent references made by the governess to people's social positions

waistcoats: sleeveless jackets, often richly embroidered

hung fire: held back, waited

Chapter Six

The governess thinks about what she has seen that day and about her later discussions of it with Mrs Grose. Mrs Grose has not seen the ghost, but, at this point in the story, has faith in the governess. She agrees that Peter Quint is after the children. The governess decides to offer herself as an 'expiatory victim' to save the children. She wonders why the children have never mentioned the former governess or valet; for Mrs Grose has told her that for a time, while he was alive, Peter Quint was in complete charge of the children. This circumstance distressed Mrs Grose, for Quint was a bad man and too free with his superiors. But Mrs Grose was too afraid of Quint to tell the master.

The next day, Monday, the governess learns that Quint had died from a wound to his head; one night, after leaving a public house, a bar, probably drunk, he had slipped on an icy hillside. But, she also discovers, there had been strange secrets and vices in his life which might suggest a more sinister cause of death.

The governess begins to think that she has been called to a heroic duty, and that the master will someday come to appreciate her for it. She must protect and defend these helpless and innocent children; it is her great chance. She fears that her excitement might become madness if it lasts too long. But it does not, for something else occurs.

One sunny afternoon, she is sitting with Flora beside a small lake on the grounds. Without looking up, she suddenly becomes aware that someone is watching them from across the lake, someone who has no right to be there. She looks at Flora, expecting a sound of surprise from her, but Flora has become strangely quiet. She is busy making a boat from two pieces of wood. The governess turns, then, to face the apparition.

COMMENTARY: There are several crucial points in this chapter. First, we find out more about the man on the tower and are assured that he really is a ghost. He is a 'bad' man, who, in life, had a great deal to do with the children. Again, several questions come up: How, exactly, did Quint die? The governess hints at something more than a mere slip on the ice. Also, why have the children never mentioned him?

Second, a sort of romance is developing in the governess's imagination, with herself as heroine and saviour of the children and with the master as hero. She is still thinking of some way to attract his attention to her, to make him admire her. She almost welcomes the opportunity provided by the ghosts.

The final event of importance in this chapter is the strange appearance of another ghost. This ghost presents another 'turn' in the mystery. The last paragraph should be examined carefully. Flora's apparent unawareness of the ghost will be significant when we discuss the meaning of the tale.

NOTES AND GLOSSARY:

liability:	openness to, tending to
consternation:	amazement and fear
prostrate:	weak and exhausted
a little service:	a little ceremony, like a church service
mutual . . . pledges:	promises to each other
impugning:	questioning or doubting as probably false
portentous:	indicating something significant about to happen, especially something bad
read into the facts:	see in the facts something not clearly there

expiatory victim:	an offering to make up for something bad; the governess will offer herself to the ghosts to keep the children safe from them
sinister:	threatening evil; bad
importunate:	pushing or demanding
listless:	not interested in anything
sinecure:	an office or job requiring little or no work; the governess's part in the children's games is such a job
Sea of Azof:	a sea north-east of the Black Sea, connected with it by the Kerch Strait, and bounded on all sides by Russia; the governess and Flora are learning geography by pretending the lake is the Sea of Azof
small clock of my courage:	the governess thinks of her courage as a clock that has not yet reached the right time to allow her to act

Chapter Seven

Two hours later, the governess gets hold of Mrs Grose, but she is only able to cry out that Flora saw the ghost. She is now convinced that the children know about the ghosts but pretend that they do not. She is amazed that an eight-year-old child can conceal her knowledge so cleverly.

She describes the figure to Mrs Grose; it was a pale woman dressed in black, who is horrible and evil—Miss Jessel, the former governess. The ghost looked only at Flora, and her eyes revealed her strong desire to get hold of the girl. The governess believes that Flora knows all this but will tell them nothing.

Mrs Grose explains that there was 'something between' the ungentlemanly and depraved Peter Quint and Miss Jessel, who was above him in social class. Quint was a low person who had his way with women. Mrs Grose does not know how Miss Jessel died. But she does know the reason Miss Jessel left Bly, and she can imagine what happened later. They both imagine something dreadful.

The governess despairs over the fate of the children, who she feels are lost.

COMMENTARY: The mystery takes several new 'turns': The governess begins to believe that the children are involved with the ghosts, and she finds out about the relationship between Quint and Jessel. The governess's thoughts spin around with each new revelation, as the situation becomes deeper and more complex. That is, she seems to become increasingly nervous, although she frequently insists on her clarity and self-control.

As usual, there is a certain amount of ambiguity in this new knowledge; for example, it is suggested, but never clearly stated, that Miss Jessel became pregnant, left Bly for that reason, and died in childbirth or in some worse way. It is left to the reader to imagine what this might have been.

Both the governess and Mrs Grose place great emphasis on the low social status of Quint as compared with that of Miss Jessel. The governess may feel that this difference in class reflects on her own social status. For, as was frequently stated in the literature of the time, governesses held a rather ambiguous and lonely social position; they were above the servants, but below their employers. A relationship between a governess and a servant would indeed be considered an 'abasement', or a lowering, on her part.

NOTES AND GLOSSARY:

fought out the interval: struggled along during the time period

stupefaction: a state of being dulled, as if by a blow or a shock; astonished

'we must keep our heads': they must keep control of themselves; the governess is constantly afraid of losing her self-control

fury of intention: strong intention

in mourning: showing deep sorrow by wearing black

a hound: a dog; a low, hateful person

Chapter Eight

Late that night, the governess and Mrs Grose review the events. The governess convinces Mrs Grose that she could not have been imagining the ghosts, for she had been able to describe Quint and Jessel clearly, even though she had never seen them before. The governess is no longer afraid for herself, but she finds her new suspicions about the children unbearable. Yet she cannot get over her feeling that Flora saw the ghost of Miss Jessel and that she took great care to make the governess think she had not.

Mrs Grose admits that Quint and Miles were always together. At one time, Mrs Grose had reminded Miles not to forget his social position by associating with a lowly servant. But Miles would often lie about where he had been. Moreover, Miles was obviously aware of the immoral relationship between Quint and Jessel, though he never spoke of it. Mrs Grose does not want to admit that Miles is bad, for she is clearly devoted to him. But she does confess that, when she spoke to him about seeing too much of Quint, Miles was unusually impudent and insulting to her.

COMMENTARY: The governess pushes the unwilling Mrs Grose to reveal more and more. Part of her desire to *know* all is based on the governess's belief that she already *does* know. She leads Mrs Grose to confirm opinions she has already formed, for example, as to the relationship between the ghosts and the children. By this time, the governess is suspicious of the children, yet she still rejects her own feelings, for neither she—nor the reader—can see anything they have done for which they might be blamed.

NOTES AND GLOSSARY:

abjure: deny

to sound (depths): to measure how deep something is

to asseverate: to declare or state positively

brushed my brow like the wing of a bat: the sense of what she does not know seems to come to the governess like a bat's wing brushing her forehead; bats are often associated with darkness, evil, death

giving the last jerk to the curtain: the governess expresses, metaphorically, her determination to discover all from Mrs Grose, to pull back suddenly on the 'curtain' with which Mrs Grose conceals her knowledge

wretches: very bad, unhappy or unfortunate persons

a fiend: a devil; a devilishly cruel or wicked person

little natural man: man as he is in nature, without the refinements and decencies of civilisation.

Chapter Nine

Days pass and nothing happens. The governess wonders if the children suspect that she thinks strange and interesting things about them. They seem unusually fond of her and try to please and entertain her. They are remarkably capable and intelligent. She realises that she should send the clever Miles back to school, but she does nothing. Only later will she realise that Miles's extraordinary intelligence might be the result of some outside influence. The children never complain or quarrel, but she does suspect that occasionally her pupils conspire against her; one keeps her busy while the other slips away.

One evening, she has not gone to bed but is sitting up reading a novel, *Amelia* (1751), by Henry Fielding (1707–1754) while Flora sleeps. Suddenly, she has a sense of something astir, moving, in the house. She takes a candle and leaves the room, locking the door. On the landing of the staircase, she sees Peter Quint. He again fixes her with his eyes, but she stands her ground, and he finally turns his back and descends the stairs into the darkness.

COMMENTARY: The governess, perhaps by accident, lets us know that she thinks the ghosts make the children 'more interesting'. The ghosts have, then, a certain positive value—they help her—in her romanticising of her own duties and of the children themselves. Here again, the governess remarks on the perfection and intelligence of the children, but she is beginning to question it.

However, just as she is beginning to feel again at peace, she sees the ghost of Peter Quint for the third time. This time, his appearance is most sinister, for he is now inside the house—another 'turn of the screw' of horror.

NOTES AND GLOSSARY:

a kind of brush of the sponge: an erasure, here referring to her forgetfulness

keeping them in the dark: preventing them from knowing the truth

preternaturally: as though outside nature; abnormally

charades: a guessing game in which the meanings of words are acted out

the brightest thread in the pensive embroidery: the governess pictures her thoughts as an embroidery, a design sewn into cloth with coloured thread; this metaphor suggests the complexity of her thoughts in which one 'thread' stands out, her thoughts about Miles's intelligence

confabulations: talks together; discussions

Fielding's 'Amelia': a novel by Henry Fielding, published in 1751, about a young married woman caught up in a network of intrigue and mistaken motives

casement: a window opening on hinges like a door

to reckon with: to deal with

Chapter Ten

When the governess returns to the room, Flora is not in bed, though she has drawn the covers up to make it appear as though she is. Flora innocently ducks down from behind the window curtains. She throws herself affectionately on the governess's lap and explains that she was looking for the governess outside in the grounds. The governess believes that Flora is lying, but she does not accuse her.

For many nights after this, the governess does not sleep, but steals out now and then to watch the staircase. One night she recognises Miss Jessel, her body bowed and her face in her hands in an attitude of sorrow. The apparition quickly vanishes.

On the eleventh night after she has seen Quint on the stairs, she wakes up suddenly at about one o'clock. Flora is again gazing out the window, so intently that she does not notice the governess go out of the room. The governess thinks that Flora is communicating with the ghost of Miss Jessel.

She goes into a room in the tower to see for herself. Peering out of the window, she sees a figure on the lawn, who is staring at something on the top of the tower. She is sickened to realise that it is 'poor little Miles himself'.

COMMENTARY: By now, the governess is fully convinced that the children communicate with the ghosts. They are not so innocent as they appear to be. Her growing awareness that reality is not always what it appears to be provides another 'turn of the screw' for the governess and the reader, who participates in the events along with her.

The governess confesses that she is becoming increasingly nervous. She hardly sleeps at night, but spends her time ghost-hunting and her days carefully watching the children, almost as though she *wants* to discover something wrong.

Up to now, she has avoided accusing the children, probably for good reason; for, as we have seen, she has nothing to accuse them of. All their behaviour seems perfectly natural, and they are able to give fairly reasonable explanations for it, as Flora does. In fact, in Chapter Ten, the governess does not see Miss Jessel; she says that Flora does. But it is Miles who is on the lawn. The governess then assumes that he is looking at someone on the tower—but is he? Again we are left in doubt.

NOTES AND GLOSSARY:

counterpane:	a cover for a bed
candour:	frankness, honesty
blanched:	turned white
Mrs Marcet:	Jane Marcet (1769–1858) wrote textbooks for elementary school children
perilously skirted:	got dangerously close
halter:	a rope for fastening horses; here, used metaphorically; the governess will put a halter on the mystery, will control it by her courage
prowling:	creeping slowly, like a hunting animal

Chapter Eleven

The next day the governess tells Mrs Grose about the incident. She is sure that Mrs Grose believes her story but does not accept her suspicions about the children. She knows that Mrs Grose is beginning to worry about her.

That afternoon, toward the end of the summer, the two women are

talking as they watch the children strolling together. The governess takes
pride in Mrs Grose's recognition of her superiority, her 'authority'. She
describes what had happened the night before. She had brought Miles
back into the house, thinking that now he would surely confess. But she
realised that she must not bring up the subject herself. However, when
she asked him what he was doing outside, Miles sweetly claimed that
he and Flora had arranged to play a trick on her. He wanted to show
her that he can be 'bad'. The governess does not believe him and thinks
that she has fallen into a trap.

COMMENTARY: Through the eyes of the governess, we now see the
'angelic' children as somewhat sinister. She fears that they are only pretending to be good to conceal their relationship with the ghosts. Yet
much of the governess's understanding is really only a matter of intuition; she *feels*, *senses*, *believes*, but at this point she actually *knows*
very little. Her doubts are revealed in her need to reassure herself that
Mrs Grose believes her story. The questions build up: Are the children
lying? What do the ghosts want? What must the governess do to save
the children?

NOTES AND GLOSSARY:

visibly blighted: noticeably ruined or destroyed

haggard: wild looking from suffering or worry

Flights of fancy gave place, in her mind, to a steady fireside glow: the
governess's imaginative speculations are replaced
in Mrs Grose's mind with a pleasant, steady, comfortable view of things

a receptacle for lurid things: a container for terrible, wild or sensational
things

witch's broth: a soup made by a witch for magical purposes,
usually thought of as containing disgusting in-
gredients

hovered: waited uncertainly

inscrutable: not easily understood

how the deuce: a slang expression used to strengthen a question

He 'had' me indeed, and in a cleft stick: the governess feels that she is
caught, or held immovable, by Quint, as in the two
halves of a split stick, tightly

under fire: under a strong verbal attack

Chapter Twelve

The next morning, the governess and Mrs Grose again watch the
children. The governess tries to explain to Mrs Grose her conviction

that the children and the ghosts perpetually meet. Even now, Miles is only pretending to read to Flora, but actually they are talking about Quint and Jessel. She knows she sounds crazy, but she is sure that the children's unearthly beauty, their 'unnatural goodness' is a 'game', a 'fraud'. The children, she insists, want only to get to Quint and Jessel. The ghosts come to 'ply' the children with evil and to entice them, until the children perish in the attempt to reach them.

Mrs Grose suggests that the children's uncle should be told, but the governess refuses. She imagines that he will regard her with derision and will see that she has simply been trying to attract his attention to herself. She threatens to leave if Mrs Grose should notify him.

COMMENTARY: The practical, sensible Mrs Grose refuses to accept the governess's fantastic theories about the children; however, she still believes the governess's claims about the ghosts, though she herself has not seen them.

The governess is more and more convinced she is right; and more and more, she regards herself as the children's saviour. Yet her thoughts about herself and the children are never separated completely from her feelings for their uncle. She must do this alone—to please him.

NOTES AND GLOSSARY:

steeped in their vision: *steeped* means soaked or completely wet; the children's vision of the dead is so strong and absorbing, it is as if they were soaked in it

lucid: clear

ply: persistently offer something

Laws!: an exclamation of surprise

scoundrels: unprincipled, dishonourable people; villains

derision: mockery, ridicule, contempt

slighted charms: neglected attractions

Chapter Thirteen

This suspense lasts for a month. The governess is sure that this has not all been due to her imagination. By a kind of tacit agreement, she and the children never speak of the subject openly. The children, in fact, seem to be most interested in hearing about her, her family, her life at home—a safe subject. But she always suspects that she is being secretly watched.

Summer is now over and autumn has begun. The sky is grey and the trees are bare; dead leaves cover the ground. The governess continues to look for the ghosts, but does not see them. She notes briefly that it has not yet been definitely proved that the children see the ghosts, but she remains convinced that the visitors *are* present, though unseen, and that the children are aware of them. At times, she wants to accuse the children, but she cannot bring herself to name the ghosts to them. But sometimes a sudden stillness, 'a pause of all life', tells her that the ghosts are there.

The children speak a great deal about their uncle. They want him to come to live with them, but the governess knows that he will not. He never writes to them or to her. She interprets this neglect as a sign of his special respect for her abilities. Although the children write to him, she lets them know that the letters are never mailed.

The governess is amazed that, in spite of her tension, she never loses patience with the children or comes to hate them. But a change is to happen.

COMMENTARY: In this chapter, the governess thinks about the quiet days that pass after the midnight incident with Miles in Chapter Ten. The coming of the gray and dreary months of autumn parallels her changed attitude toward the children. When she came, in June, they seemed like angels; now, they seem like demons pretending to be angels. Everything they do, their affection for her, their interest in her life, arouses her suspicions—suspicions that she herself refers to as an obsession.

But she never names Quint and Jessel to the children. By this time the reader may have begun to wonder if she is proceeding correctly in this matter. For example, her refusal to mail the children's letters to their uncle reflects her desire to do her duty perfectly, as he ordered it, but it also suggests a kind of selfishness on her part, a desire to keep the children all to herself.

NOTES AND GLOSSARY:

infernal: hellish, devilish

tacit: unspoken, but understood

alleys that we perceived to be blind: small passages between buildings that are closed at one end; their conversation turns into directions in which they may not continue (for fear of naming the ghosts)

Goody Gosling's celebrated 'mot': the well-known saying of Goody Gosling, possibly a servant in the governess's home

withered garlands: strings or circles of flowers, now dried up and dying

consummation: completion, fulfilment

blasphemous: irreverent, impious; against God

obsession: a dominating feeling or idea that the person cannot escape from

palpable: easily seen, heard, or touched; obvious

vociferously: loudly

Though they were not angels, they 'passed', as the French say: refers to a common folk belief that a lull or a silence in a conversation is caused by angels passing; here, it is the ghosts who 'pass', causing 'a stillness, a pause of all life'

festal: related to a feast or celebration

Chapter Fourteen

The governess, the children, and Mrs Grose are walking to church together one frosty Sunday morning. The governess begins to wonder why the children never resent her constant attention to them.

Then, she thinks, 'the curtain rose on the last act of my dreadful drama'. Miles pipes up innocently to ask when he will be going back to school. With this, she feels that a new issue has come up between them. He tells her that he is a growing boy, who should not spend all his time with women. He mentions how good he has been, but hints that he *can* be bad.

Mrs Grose and Flora are already in the church. Miles asks the governess, 'Does my uncle think what *you* think?' She is confused, but he merely wants to know if his uncle realises he is growing up. She replies that she does not think his uncle cares very much. Miles suggests that maybe he can be made to care, if he comes to Bly. Miles says that he will get his uncle to come; and he marches on alone into the church.

COMMENTARY: On first reading, this chapter may not seem nearly so significant as, say, Chapter Thirteen, in which the ghost of Quint first appears, but we have the governess's word that it is the turning point in the story. Though not the climax, the high point of the story, it is the beginning of the resolution of the complicated situation that has gradually been built up.

There are several significant points to note here. First, the governess admits to herself that she has become like a gaoler to the children. This thought is related to a new 'turn' in the story, Miles's request to return to school. In spite of what the governess has been thinking of the relationship between the children and the ghosts, Miles is, in fact, expressing a normal desire to be with other boys like himself and to get away from Bly, which presumably means, also, away from the ghosts. Moreover, the governess does not bring up Miles's dismissal from school, and he seems to be completely unaware of it.

The governess's discussion with Miles about his uncle is typically ambiguous; much of what is said may have a double meaning. For example, when Miles asks if his uncle *knows*, the governess first thinks he is referring to what she knows about the ghosts. But then we discover that he is simply talking about his growing up. The importance of *knowing* is heavily emphasised in the tale, as the governess tells it. She continually wonders what the children *know*—about her, about the ghosts —and she is continually striving, herself, to *know* more. Thus, the tale is, in a sense, about her own growing knowledge.

Finally, this chapter clearly reveals the governess's continued resistance to letting the children communicate with their uncle. Now she is faced with a new 'turn'—the prospect of Miles's insistence that his uncle come, even if he has to bring him himself—a prospect she dreads.

NOTES AND GLOSSARY:

inexorable:	relentless, persistent, that which cannot be avoided
abysmal:	like an abyss, too deep to measure
pipe:	a high piercing voice, like that of a child
intonations:	the sound patterns or melody of the voice in speaking
made one 'catch':	made one understand
pew:	a benchlike seat in a church
hassock:	a cushion used as a footstool or for kneeling in church
venial:	not serious as a sin; excusable, forgivable

Chapter Fifteen

The governess remains alone outside the church, thinking about what Miles has said. She admits to herself that she must take some action concerning Miles's schooling and that his uncle should come and deal with the problem. But she finds it surprisingly 'unnatural' that Miles, a mere boy, has consciously planned to force her into this unpleasant position.

Waiting outside the church, she suddenly realises that she can avoid the whole problem by simply running away now, while everyone is occupied. She returns to the house, tormented by her doubts. Going into the schoolroom to collect her things, she sees Miss Jessel seated at her desk. The ghost rises in a detached and melancholy way—'dishonoured and tragic'. The governess cries out to her and she vanishes, leaving the governess with a conviction that she must remain at Bly.

COMMENTARY: Again, the governess thinks over what has happened. She now admits her fear of bringing the issue into the open.

This is the third time she sees the ghost of Miss Jessel (first, on the lake, in Chapter Six, and then on the stair at midnight, in Chapter Ten). It is also the first time she has spoken to one of the ghosts—a new 'twist' in the story—and her doing so causes the figure to vanish.

NOTES AND GLOSSARY:

spectre: a spirit, ghost, apparition
reeled: fell back, as under a blow or shock
her identity flared up: Miss Jessel's identity suddenly became apparent
                     to the governess, as if a fire blazed up before her
vile: morally low, wretched, degraded, hateful

Chapter Sixteen

The same Sunday, Mrs Grose and the children return from church. The children do not ask about her absence from church, and the governess suspects that they know.

She tells Mrs Grose about having seen Miss Jessel, who, she says, suffers the torments of the damned and wants to share them with Flora. However, she has finally decided to send for the children's uncle, even though she fears he will reproach her for having done nothing about Miles's schooling. Again, the two women speculate about what Miles might have done at school. The governess asserts that it was some 'wickedness' that he learned from Quint and Jessel. After more discussion, she decides to write to the uncle that night.

COMMENTARY: This brief chapter contains an important decision on the part of the governess—to contact her employer. This decision indicates her readiness, finally, to take some action to bring this unnatural situation to an end.

NOTES AND GLOSSARY:

garnished: decorated
rueful: sorrowful, repentant; sorry that something has
                 been done
candour: frankness, honesty
bailiff: the overseer or supervisor of a large estate like Bly

Chapter Seventeen

The evening of the same Sunday, the weather has changed. The governess is sitting before a blank sheet of paper listening to the wind and the rain. Finally, she takes a candle, and goes to stand at Miles's door; for her obsession compels her to find out if he is resting or not.

He gaily calls to her to come in. She wonders suspiciously how he knew she was there, but he tells her that she was very noisy. He has been thinking, he says, of their 'queer business', of the way she brings him up and 'all the rest'. She feels that there is something fantastic in their relationship. She begins to press him indirectly for information about what he did at school. But instead, he complains that he wants to get away from Bly, that his uncle must come, and she must settle things with him. He almost accuses her — she will have much to explain to his uncle. In turn, she points out that he too will have much to explain, but Miles seems to be completely ignorant of what she means.

She is so impressed with his cheerfulness and bravery in putting off her questions that she embraces him, again asking him if he has anything to tell her. He replies that he wants her to leave him alone. She thinks that she has not meant to harass him, but that to abandon him now would be to lose him. She tells him that she has begun a letter to his uncle and again questions him about school. He seems to be giving in slightly, and she embraces him once more; she cries out passionately that she wants to help him. She would rather die, she says, than give him pain.

Suddenly, she feels she has said too much. Though the window is closed, there is a sudden blast of cold air, and Miles shrieks loudly. The candle has gone out.

COMMENTARY: The change in the weather corresponds to a new turn of events. A strange and intense relationship seems to have built up between Miles and the governess. Miles wants to go off to school, but she is afraid of 'losing' him (although it may occur to the reader that this would be the best way to get him away from the ghost of Quint). She is still obsessed with the idea that if the children can be made to confess, they can somehow be 'saved'. But for all her efforts, she learns nothing.

As often happens in this tale, their conversation is full of double meanings; for example, Miles refers to 'this queer business of ours'; he could mean her tight control of his life or he could mean the 'ghostly business'. Like the governess, the reader is puzzled as to how much Miles knows.

NOTES AND GLOSSARY:

troop of cavalry: a group of soldiers on horseback

his little resources taxed to play ... a part of innocence: Miles 'taxed his resources', used his abilities to the fullest, to pretend to be innocent

unimpeachable: cannot be questioned or accused

poignancy: the state of being distressing to the emotions

harass: to trouble

Chapter Eighteen

The next day, the governess has in her pocket the letter she has written to the children's uncle. The children are particularly exemplary in their lessons that day, especially Miles, and she thinks how frank and free he seems. But she has been 'initiated', that is, given special knowledge, and is now aware that although he seems innocent, he has had 'the imagination of all evil'. She only hopes that he has never *done* anything evil.

After lunch, Miles plays the piano for her, so beautifully that she falls into a daydream. Suddenly, she becomes aware that Flora is not with them. Miles claims that he does not know where she is. She and Mrs Grose frantically search the house for Flora, but without success. Finally, it occurs to the governess that Miles has played a devilish trick on her to keep her attention so that Flora can go out to be with Miss Jessel. Now Miles is able to be alone with Quint in the schoolroom. Before going out with Mrs Grose to find Flora, she quickly puts the letter on the hall table for Luke, a servant, to take to town.

COMMENTARY: Again, the governess is torn between the apparent innocence and cleverness of the children and what she knows about their tricks and their evil companions. Miles, she thinks, has enchanted her into relaxing her constant watching of him and Flora.

NOTES AND GLOSSARY:

exemplary: good enough to imitate, serving as a model or pattern

David playing to Saul: this refers to the story in the Bible in which the young David, later to become king of Israel, plays his harp to refresh and soothe King Saul, who is tormented by an evil spirit: 1 Samuel 16:19

tantamount: equivalent, equal

incoherent: disconnected

I . . . also looked volumes: the governess looked at Mrs Grose in such a way that her look seemed to have as much meaning as many volumes of books

demurred: objected, hesitated

Chapter Nineteen

The governess and Mrs Grose hurry to the lake, for the governess believes that Flora may have gone there. They notice that the boat has disappeared. Circling the lake, they find the boat hidden out of sight, and they marvel that Flora was able to move it by herself.

Passing through a gate, they see Flora, smiling at them innocently. As they go up to her, she bends down silently and picks up a piece of ugly, withered fern, as if she had come there just for it. She has come out of the copse, a small group of trees near the lake. Mrs Grose embraces

Flora, who peeps seriously over her shoulder at the governess and drops the fern, as if there were no longer any point in pretending.

Flora innocently asks them why they are not properly dressed and where Miles is. The governess has a sudden burst of courage. She replies to Flora, 'I'll tell you if you'll tell *me* . . . Where, my pet, is Miss Jessel?'

COMMENTARY: This is a significant chapter. The children finally manage to get away from the governess for a few minutes. We realise how unnaturally closely she has been watching them all these weeks. Moreover, in this chapter, the governess, for the first time, mentions the name of one of the ghosts to one of the children. Having written the letter to the children's uncle, she is now taking another decisive step towards dealing with the sitation.

NOTES AND GLOSSARY:

She had not given me the slip: she had not got away from me

appal: overcome with fear, fill with horror

prodigious feat: an extraordinary achievement

I . . . had panted to too many livelier measures: literally, I had breathed hard dancing to many faster pieces of music; an analogy in which the governess indicates that she is not surprised at what Flora has done because she has seen so many greater wonders before this

withered fern: a plant with large leaves and small stem which is drying up because it is winter

flagrantly ominous: obviously and openly threatening evil

dumb convulsion: silent muscular contraction of the body

in a flash like the glitter of a drawn blade, the jostle of the cup that my hand . . . had held high: the governess indicates that she is now ready to act; the image of the full cup is commonly used by James to indicate the completion of something; but this image may also suggest the lance and grail, the cup from which Christ drank at the Last Supper before his crucifixion; these were the objects of a holy search in the mythical stories of King Arthur and his knights; thus, the governess suggests her sense of a kind of holy duty towards the children

Chapter Twenty

On mentioning the name of Miss Jessel, the governess notices a stricken look on Flora's face. Mrs Grose shrieks. And then, across the lake, where she had stood before, Miss Jessel appears. The governess feels joyful that she now has proof that she is 'neither cruel nor mad'.

She is startled, however, to see Flora looking, not at the ghost, but at her, seriously and with disapproval. Even worse, Mrs Grose cannot see the ghost, and the governess feels her proof crumble. Flora and Mrs Grose draw together, united against her. The governess no longer sees Flora as a beautiful little princess but as someone common and ugly, especially when Flora cries out, 'I see nobody. I see nothing. I never *have*. I think you're cruel. I don't like you!' Her manner reminds the governess of a vulgar street girl. Flora then turns to Mrs Grose and begs to be taken away from the governess.

The governess realises that she had made a terrible mistake by speaking. Flora, with Miss Jessel's help, has tricked her, and she knows she has lost Flora for ever.

Flora and Mrs Grose leave her, and she remains by the pool sobbing. When she gets back to the house, she finds that Flora's things have been removed from her room. Flora spends the night with Mrs Grose, and the governess does not see her again. But at eight o'clock, Miles comes to sit silently with her; now that he has truly won his freedom, he wants to be with her.

COMMENTARY: In this chapter, Miss Jessel appears for the fourth and final time. The governess's joy that she has proof for her suspicions suggests that she has not really been sure of herself all along. In any case, it is a 'dreadful turn' for her to discover that Mrs Grose cannot see the ghost. Yet she is convinced that Flora does see it and that her denial is a dramatic display designed to 'take in', or fool, Mrs Grose. Thus, as the story progresses, the governess gradually sees the children as almost supernaturally clever as they act under the direction of the ghosts. Yet the reader should note that up to this point the children have never shown any sign of having seen the ghosts.

NOTES AND GLOSSARY:

smitten:	as if struck by a blow or affected by strong feeling
ravenous demon:	greedy devil
feign:	pretend
reprobation:	disapproval
formidably:	as if inspiring fear of failure; strongly
groan of negation:	a deep, unhappy sound, indicating her denial
blundering in:	coming in, in a clumsy or awkward way
vulgarly pert:	bold, forward, in a vulgar or common way
so grotesque a false note:	a musical note that is badly off key, does not suit the tune; here, anything that does not fit into the situation
consternation:	amazement and fear
the ebbing actual:	the flowing backward or fading of the genuine
material testimony:	physical proof or evidence

Chapter Twenty-one

At dawn the next day, Mrs Grose wakes the governess with the news that Flora has had a restless night. She has continually insulted the governess and denies that she has ever seen any ghosts. The governess remarks that Flora and Miss Jessel have been very clever; they will make the uncle think that she is a low person, so that Flora can get rid of her. The governess directs Mrs Grose to take Flora and go to the children's uncle, but to leave Miles at Bly alone with her. The governess believes that Miles wants to speak to her, and will if given more time.

Mrs Grose is anxious to go, for, she says, she has heard Flora say terrible things, 'horrors', which she must have learned from Quint and Jessel. The governess is relieved to hear this, for, she says, 'It so justifies me!' Because of Flora's shocking language, Mrs Grose now believes the governess's suspicions are true, in spite of the fact that she has never seen the ghosts herself.

Furthermore, Mrs Grose reluctantly informs the governess that the letter she wrote to the uncle disappeared from the table before Luke could take it to town. They realise that Miles has stolen it. Mrs Grose is particularly distressed at this evidence of Miles's dishonesty. The governess says that the letter was nothing but a request for an interview; she believes that Miles will confess, and, 'If he confesses, he's saved.' And if Miles is saved, then so is she.

COMMENTARY: Mrs Grose now believes the governess, for the children have finally provided evidence of evil—Flora by her shocking language and Miles by his stealing of the letter—another 'turn' in the story. This is the first concrete evidence that the children have, as the governess insists, been 'corrupted'. The governess is still obsessed with the idea that the children must confess in order to be saved.

But she also wants to be 'saved', at least in the opinion of her employer. Again, the desire to please her employer provides a strong motive for her actions in regard to the children. She is pleased to have the support and the good word of Mrs Grose.

However, we are never told exactly what Flora says. The age in which James wrote the story, the end of the nineteenth century, would not permit the frankness of expression that we find in stories written today, nor would a proper lady of that time have repeated shocking language. But it is typical of this story that evil is only suggested, never stated directly.

NOTES AND GLOSSARY:

girded her loins: put on a belt, or armed herself; an expression meaning that she prepared herself for action

chit: an impertinent or disrespectful young person
I did put my foot in it: a common expression meaning to say the wrong thing, to say something by mistake that may bring unfortunate consequences
repudiate: deny
winced: drew back, as if in pain
sequestration: removal or banishment; seclusion
evocation: calling up, as of a thought or memory
plumb: a weight used to measure depth; Mrs Grose and the governess are making 'mutual soundings'; Mrs Grose is the first to bring up the 'plumb'; that is, she is the first to speak

Chapter Twenty-two

Flora and Mrs Grose depart that same day. Miles does not come in for lessons, and the governess does not look for him. He has his freedom now, she thinks, and will keep it.

She is overcome with doubts and fears and spends the day in walks about the house. Her sanity and her success will depend on her strong will to forget how unnatural all this is; she must try to think of it as 'only another turn of the screw of ordinary human virtue'. She hopes she can depend on Miles's remarkable intelligence to save him.

At dinner, he asks about Flora, but she replies that Flora has simply become ill and has had to go away from Bly. Their meal is brief, and they say little until after the servants clear the table, when Miles turns and remarks, 'Well—so we're alone'.

COMMENTARY: The title of the story is mentioned for the second time in the tale. (It was first mentioned in the Prologue.) Here, it expresses the governess's hope that she can regard all the strange events as somewhat natural, as simply another twist of the ordinary.

The governess unhappily accepts the fact that Miles now feels perfectly free of her, free to follow his own will. Yet the final scene of the governess and Miles alone after dinner reveals a strange sense of intimacy, of closeness, between them. Here, quite naturally and genuinely, he seems to return the special affection she has always felt for him.

NOTES AND GLOSSARY:
face to face with the elements: confronting the weather, the atmospheric forces; an expression which indicates that she faces the basic situation
clutching the helm: holding tightly to the steering mechanism of a ship; again, as in Chapter One, the governess thinks of herself as guiding a ship

perambulations: walks
pomp: dignified display, magnificence
specious: deceptive
wrest: twist or pull away by force
dissipate: scatter, disperse
grossness of admonition: the unpleasantness or vulgarity of having to reprove or blame
whimsically: as if from a sudden fancy; capriciously

Chapter Twenty-three

They are not completely alone, they agree; they have 'the others'. Miles stands staring out of the window at the dull November day, with his back to the governess. He is looking for something he cannot see—the first time, she thinks, that such a failure has occurred for him.

She tells him that she now accepts his independence from her, but she has stayed at Bly because she wants him to tell her something. He begins to look fearful, and she is sorry to have to force him to admit guilt. He starts to go out, promising he will tell her everything, but later; first he has to see Luke. It is another lie, and she regrets it, except that, she thinks, his lies prove her suspicions to be true. She asks one thing before he goes out—that he should tell her if, yesterday, he took the letter from the hall table.

COMMENTARY: Again, this chapter contains ambiguous references and allusions. 'The others', of which they speak, might refer to the servants or to the ghosts.

The governess believes that Miles is showing signs of breaking down; he seems to make a sort of half-confession—he *has* been concealing something from her. Notice the satisfaction of the governess when the children actually do something bad, thus supporting her terrible suspicions. By this point in the story, Miles has become unsure, nervous, 'quivering', as well as the governess. The governess's question leads directly into the following chapter. We are nearing the climax, the high point of the tale.

NOTES AND GLOSSARY:
cogitating: thinking hard
with all accommodation: with full agreement, forgetting of differences
a gloss: a misleading interpretation
impertinence: unmannerly presumption or boldness, insolence
tone: a particular way of speaking to express a special meaning
a perverse horror: a horror that persists in spite of her knowing it is wrong

So we circled . . . like fighters not daring to close: they moved around each other like fighters afraid to get near each other and begin fighting

---

Chapter Twenty-four

As she asks the question, the governess sees the ghost of Peter Quint at the window. But Miles's back is toward the window, and the governess determines to keep him unaware, to pretend no one is there: 'It was like fighting with a demon for a human soul . . .'

Yes, Miles confesses, he took the letter and read it. She embraces him joyfully and can feel the strong beating of his heart. The figure remains at the window; she is elated since Miles is unaware it is present.

The governess again looks at the window and sees that the figure has gone. She feels that she has won—she shall 'get *all*' from Miles. Though he has surrendered completely to her, she continues to press him with questions, for she has become 'blind with victory'.

Yet, momentarily, she is overcome by the sudden fear that he may really be innocent, for, she thinks, 'if he *were* innocent, what then on earth was *I*?' She lets go of him, and he turns toward the window, now clear. He tells her that at school he 'said things' to the other boys, who must have repeated them; the masters found out, and he was dismissed.

As she continues to question him, Quint reappears at the window. She senses a weakening of her victory, a renewed battle. Her sudden embrace makes Miles guess that something is wrong. But she realises that he cannot see the ghost of Quint. She cries out to the ghost, 'No more, no more, no more!'

Miles then asks if Miss Jessel is there. The governess shows him the figure at the window, but he sees nothing. Finally, he cries out, 'Peter Quint—you devil!' But looking where she points, he sees only the 'quiet day'; the figure is gone. He cries out, and she catches and holds him. In a moment, she realises that he is dead.

COMMENTARY: Strangely enough, in this final chapter, we are left with more questions than ever. The governess does get Miles to confess—but to what? Very little, really. He has stolen the letter; he has 'said things' at school. We are never told what these things were.

This is the fourth and final appearance of Quint, whom Miles does not see. (Remember, it was the fourth appearance of Miss Jessel that brought about the final crisis between her and the governess.) It is interesting that although all the way through the tale, the governess insists that Miles has been seeing Quint, yet now, when she tells him the ghost is present, he first guesses that it is Miss Jessel. Even now, it is not clear that either of the children has ever seen the ghosts.

The governess worries that she has been incorrect in her suspicions; for, she thinks, if he is innocent, then she is guilty of a terrible wrong. But, as usual, this fear does not last long with her. She continues to pressure him, until he calls out the name of Peter Quint. This reply, which at first seems to answer all our questions and hers, is, in fact, quite ambiguous. Miles does not *see* Quint now, so supposedly this outcry is a kind of confession that he has seen him before this time. But perhaps he only guesses at what the governess expects him to say. Also, it is not clear whom he means by the words, 'you devil'. It might be Quint or the governess herself. If it is the latter, why should he refer to the governess as a 'devil'?

This outcry is the climax of the story—its highest point, in which the tension is greatest; the complication which has been built up throughout the story is brought to a head. The last few paragraphs are the *dénouement*, the final untangling of the plot. The tale ends quickly with Miles's death. There is no return to the original setting of the prologue, a fact that has puzzled many readers. Of course, such a return would weaken the strong effect of the last paragraph, in which we have the final, unexpected 'turn of the screw' of horror.

As we discuss the tale, it might be interesting to keep in mind a few of the unanswered questions that still remain with us at the end of the tale. What, exactly, is the evil that Flora and Miles learned from Quint and Jessel? Are they really saved at the end of the tale? If so, in what sense are they saved? Have the governess's interpretations of their behaviour been correct? That is, have they really seen the ghosts and communicated with them? Has the governess done anything wrong in her efforts to save the children? If so, what? And finally, why does Miles die?

NOTES AND GLOSSARY:

sentinel: one who watches, a guard

transcendently: as if going beyond ordinary circumstances or limits

a sound ... that I drank like a waft of fragrance: a sound that she heard with pleasure, as if she breathed in a pleasant smell

prowl of a baffled beast: the movement of a puzzled animal searching unsuccessfully for prey

ravage: severe damage, ruin

quenched: put an end to, ended

desolation: loneliness, dreariness; feeling of being abandoned

pathos: ability to call up pity or sympathy

a divination: an instinctive understanding

supplication: prayer, entreaty, begging

hurled over an abyss: thrown into a bottomless hole

dispossessed: no longer controlled or dominated from within by a spirit

Part 3

Commentary

The Turn of the Screw has been one of the most popular of James's works. Surprisingly, his own opinion of the work was not very high. He once referred to it as a 'pot-boiler', a work produced, without much effort, to sell quickly. His preface to the New York Edition of his works describes *The Turn of the Screw* as 'a piece of ingenuity pure and simple, of cold artistic calculation, an *amusette* to catch those not easily caught'. That is, in writing the tale, he did not hope to produce a 'great' work, but he did strive to achieve an effect on the reader—an effect of the horrible and the mysterious. Each element in the story contributes to this total effect, and, as we take the story apart for analysis, we must keep in mind that each aspect of it is significant only as an integral part of a carefully planned and unified whole.

The Prologue

One major problem an author faces in writing a tale of the supernatural is to get the reader to believe in the unbelievable and to respond to it as though it really happened. James does this, partly, in the Prologue.

The Turn of the Screw is told as a tale within a tale. That is, it is not told to the reader directly, but is introduced in the Prologue through another story, this one about a group of friends who are telling stories. We say that it is set in a 'frame'. The frame of a story, like that of a picture, has several functions: to set the story off from the real world and define its limits, to focus the reader's attention on it, and to emphasise significant aspects of it.

First, the Prologue of *The Turn of the Screw* establishes a clear boundary between the reader and the tale itself. It sets him at a psychological distance from the tale. Through it, he enters another world, unrelated to that in which he lives. He must accept it as it is and avoid trying to judge it on the basis of his own practical experience.

Second, the Prologue of *The Turn of the Screw* prepares the reader for the tale and focuses his attention on significant aspects of it. It does this in three ways. First, it prepares the reader by introducing him to the characters and providing background information about them. Second, the Prologue establishes an impression of verisimilitude, of truth to reality. Third, the Prologue introduces the atmosphere of mystery, suspense and horror which will grow as the tale progresses.

The Prologue gives the reader information. It introduces him to two groups of characters—those who are involved in telling the tale and those who take part in the tale itself. And it tells something about their backgrounds and motives. Douglas provides a link between the two groups; he has known the governess, whose story he tells, and has loved her. His interest in her and in her account arouses the reader's interest and focuses his attention on it. Douglas's high opinion of the governess and the fact that he believes her story encourages the reader to do the same.

Thus the Prologue provides the 'air of reality' which James felt was essential to fiction. The reader is not plunged at once into the mystery; instead, he is gradually drawn into it through the commonplace circumstance of a story-telling session. He accepts it, at first, because it is presented as 'just a story'. But it is a story that has been written down on an old manuscript, and thus it has a certain 'authenticity' as a true account, a history. Moreover, it happened to a real person, who is known to one of the narrators. In using such devices—the frame, the manuscript, the believing storyteller—James imitated the popular ghost story; such tricks help the reader to accept events that he might otherwise reject as fantastic or even as ridiculous.

Finally, the third function of the Prologue is to introduce the element of mystery and suspense into the story. The tale may be 'just a story', but it is told in a large, old house before a fire, on a dark, wintry night. In such a setting, we are prepared to believe almost anything. Several stories have already been told, and Douglas promises one even more gruesome than they. It took place in the past, when, as we all know, strange things were more likely to happen and less likely to be questioned. Thus, the reader is prepared to be amazed and terrified even before he begins the governess's account in Chapter One.

The governess's tale

The setting

In Chapter One, the governess travels from the world of London to the remote and isolated country house of Bly. This house and its surroundings provide the setting for the tale. It is an 'enclosed setting', for all of the events of the story take place within it. At Bly, the governess is cut off from the familiar world she knows. Even before she has arrived, she has been afraid of being lonely there, and her sense of her isolation— and the reader's sense of it—is increased by her employer's demand that she never communicate with him.

The house, as described by the governess, combines elements of the commonplace and the strange. She recognises that it is simply 'a big, ugly, antique, but convenient house'; but she is, nevertheless, astonished at its size and splendour and impressed with its possibilities for adventure and excitement. It is built like an old castle, full of 'empty chambers and dull corridors', which she goes through with Flora, 'secret by secret'. She imagines that she has entered a storybook world in which anything might happen. As Flora shows her through the house, she thinks: '. . . I had the view of a castle of romance, inhabited by a rosy sprite, such a place as would somehow . . . take all colour out of story-books and fairy-tales. Wasn't it just a storybook over which I had fallen a-doze and a-dream?'

As the story progresses, the quality of the setting seems to change; the dreamland becomes a threatening, nightmare world. The house, which at first seems so magnificent to the governess, becomes a place of treachery, terror and death. Nature itself seems to respond to the change. The governess arrives at Bly on a golden day in June. The story ends on a gray and dreary day in November. The 'bright flowers' and the 'clustered tree-tops' of Chapter One become 'withered garlands' and 'dead leaves' by Chapter Twelve. Thus, the setting itself contributes to the growing sense of mystery and horror.

The atmosphere

According to his statements in the preface, the atmosphere or feeling that James hoped to arouse in the reader was that of mystification, uncanniness, of undefinable danger. To achieve this atmosphere, he made use of a number of popular tricks often found in ghost stories, such as the setting in an isolated, old house with barren and gloomy surroundings, the unexplained appearances of ghosts, and the governess's vague sense of approaching disaster. He uses the device of the unexplained sound—soft steps by the governess's door on her first morning at Bly —and, in contrast, the sudden silences which accompany the appearances of the ghosts. James even makes use of such old tricks as the candle which suddenly blows out when there is no wind.

Yet James is able to give many of these *clichés*, these trite and overused devices of the popular ghost story, special meaning in his tale. He does so, partly, by leaving them ambiguous; we are not sure whether they are merely accidents and coincidences or they are the effect of supernatural influence. For the author is careful not to allow the reader to lose sight of reality. Except for the ghosts themselves, almost everything in the tale—the behaviour of the children, the change of seasons, the unusual sounds—can be explained as misinterpretations of natural occurrences. By refusing to be precise about these matters, James creates an air of mystery in which the danger seems greatest because it is incomprehensible and undefinable.

Thus, in creating his atmosphere, James has continued to maintain the balance between the realistic and the fantastic. James draws his reader into the world of the romance as Nathaniel Hawthorne defined it, 'somewhere between the real world and fairy-land, where the Actual and the Imaginary may meet, and each imbue itself with the nature of the other'. In *The Turn of the Screw*, the ordinary comes to seem weird and threatening; for example, the playfulness and charm of the children takes on a horrifying character as the tale progresses. On the other hand, the strange becomes normal; in Chapter Sixteen, the governess is able to make a small joke about her meeting with Miss Jessel, as if the ghost were a living person. In fact, as the story progresses, the ghosts come to seem almost natural at Bly, simply characters in the drama; their evil comes to seem simply another 'turn of the screw of human virtue', as the governess says in Chapter Twenty-two.

Point of view

The point of view of the tale is that of the first person; that is, the governess tells the story about herself, in terms of *I*, as opposed to *he* or *she*. The reader is disposed to accept her story because she is supposedly a real person who herself takes part in the events. The reader follows her into the strange world of Bly, which he views entirely through her eyes. In this sense, James is often regarded as a psychological novelist. The reader comes to know the governess through the stream of her thoughts as she strives to understand herself and the world around her. He shares her mystification, her efforts to explain the ghosts in terms of her, up to then, rather dull and ordinary experience. And the reader participates in her amazement on discovering the truth about them.

Yet sensible as she may seem at first, the governess is remarkably sensitive to the supernatural. Her account is sprinkled with such terms as 'uncanny', 'sinister', 'unnatural', 'portentous', and 'threatening'. She discovers elements of the mysterious in events which might have seemed to the reader to be perfectly normal. Thus, her responses direct his responses. She tells the reader what to think, and she reveals to him the evil hidden in the seemingly harmless and commonplace events.

The style

The fullness and richness of James's later prose style makes it possible for him to reveal the complexity of the narrator's thought, the varied level of her responses as she works them out in her own conscious mind. Readers sometimes become exasperated with the length and complexity of many of James's sentences; for example, this sentence which begins

Chapter Six, following the startling revelation that Quint is a ghost:

> It took of course more than that particular passage to place us together in presence of what we had now to live with as we could—my dreadful liability to impressions of the order so vividly exemplified, and my companion's knowledge, henceforth—a knowledge half consternation and half compassion—of that liability.

Yet in such sentences, James suggests the relationship of a number of subtle and complex ideas and conveys a sense of their deeper significance. The governess refers to her having seen the ghost of Quint, and she suggests what it means to her understanding of herself, to Mrs Grose, and to their future relationship.

Here is a suggestion: To get through such sentences, the reader should try speaking them out loud. James dictated *The Turn of the Screw* to a typist. The meaning of many difficult sentences suddenly becomes clear when they are spoken slowly and with emphasis, as he composed them.

The sentence quoted above also exemplifies the suggestiveness and indirectness which can be so worrisome to the reader of James. For example, the governess does not say that she is liable to see ghosts, but that she is liable 'to impressions of the order so vividly exemplified', referring to the appearance of Quint. This indirect wording suggests that the seeing of ghosts is only an *example* of the impressions which the governess may receive. There may be others yet to come, too subtle and deep for definition.

However, not all of the sentences are long and complex. The style is characterised by alternation—of long and difficult sentences set off and emphasised by sentences that are short, sharp and precise. Long, speculative passages are relieved by sections of tense and hurried dialogue. The effect is that of slow and worried thought which suddenly breaks into moments of excited activity. Slowly growing realisation is brought suddenly to a sharp conclusion. For example, in Chapter Thirteen, the governess thinks about those times in which she wishes to speak to the children about the ghosts, but cannot:

> After these secret scenes I chattered more than ever, going on volubly enough till one of our prodigious, palpable hushes occurred—I can call them nothing else—the strange, dizzy lift or swim (I try for terms!) into a stillness, a pause of all life, that had nothing to do with the more or less noise that at the moment we might be engaged in making and that I could hear through any deepened exhilaration or quickened recitation or louder strum of the piano. Then it was that the others, the outsiders, were there.

In the first sentence above, the governess suggests her growing awareness of the strange silences that sometimes come upon them. The second sentence states, concisely and directly, her knowledge of what those silences mean.

Plot and structure

The plot, or story, of *The Turn of the Screw* follows the simple pattern of many ghost stories and folk tales: ghosts or demons come to carry off innocent children, while some other person tries to save them. James centres the tale on this single situation, and examines its effect on the thoughts and behaviour of the characters. He intentionally kept the story simple. In his preface he referred to *The Turn of the Screw* as a fairy tale because it is 'short and sharp and single'; that is, like a fairy tale, it has a tight, concentrated structure and a sharp, intense effect.

But in his hands, as he noted, this little story turns upon itself. This 'turning' is suggested in the title. Through a number of unexpected changes and revelations, the simple tale becomes increasingly complex. It is, in essence, a series of ironies. That is, the true meaning of the events and the true nature of the characters is not always what it appears to be on the surface; it is often, in fact, the opposite. There is irony in the fact that the governess, wishing for her employer, sees Peter Quint instead, who at first *seems* to be her employer; there is irony in the children's deceptive innocence, irony in the governess's misdirected efforts to save them. As we read, we begin to wonder what, precisely, the truth is.

James builds up these ironies through the narrative, or storytelling, technique of scenic presentation. The story progresses through a series of scenes. These scenes alternate with passages in which the governess thinks about them or discusses them. For example, in Chapter Three, Quint's first appearance on the tower is presented as though it were a single scene in a drama; we see it in our minds as a static picture rather than as a flow of action. The following chapter begins with the governess's thoughts about the event, and it ends with another such scene— that of Quint looking in at the dining-room window. Many similar scenes stand out in our minds. For example, when we finish the novel, we remember Flora as she appears in progressively changing scenes: as a sweet little fairy child showing the governess through the house, as a clever liar throwing herself on the governess's lap in her bedroom, as an ugly and vulgar brat cursing the governess by the lake. Each of these scenes is an ironic contrast to the one before it, another 'turn of the screw' of the governess's and the reader's puzzlement.

With each scene, the conflict in the story develops—between the governess and the ghosts and between the governess and the children. For example, at first, the ghost of Quint simply appears, and the governess senses something strange about him. The possibility of a conflict between him and the governess is suggested, however, on his second appearance at the dining-room window, when the governess becomes aware of his danger to the children. By the time the governess sees Miss Jessel on the lake, she is determined to battle with the ghosts. At the same time, another conflict enters the plot, involving the governess and the children. At first, she views them as little angels, but gradually she realises that they too are against her and must be defeated to be saved. Her knowledge develops slowly, step by step, scene by scene. These conflicts are resolved in the last few chapters when the governess confronts the children and the ghosts. Miles's confession and the appearance of Quint in the last chapter is the climax of the tale, the point of greatest tension.

The tale ends quickly with Miles's death. There is no return to the frame of the story, for two very good reasons. First, the Prologue has given the reader all the information that James felt was necessary to understand the tale. Second, such a return would detract from the shock of the ending of the tale. The author has gradually and carefully led the reader to forget that the tale is 'just a story'; the reader has come to know the characters and to care about their fates; he has come to believe, as they do, in the ghosts. He would feel cheated or tricked to be suddenly reminded that they are only invented figures in a story. The author has drawn the reader into a world of the incredible, the strange, the horrible; and he chooses to leave him there, to add nothing that would lessen the effect he has worked so hard to create.

The characters

The governess

Like a fairy tale, *The Turn of the Screw* involves only a few significant characters. Of these, only the governess and the children change or develop as the story progresses. The governess is the most complex character. Excepting the Prologue, the reader perceives the entire action and all the other characters of the tale solely through her eyes.

Therefore, the kind of person she is becomes vitally important to an understanding of the tale. She is young and pretty, probably about twenty years old when the events occur; she is the daughter of a poor country parson. No doubt she was strictly brought up according to the rigid standards of nineteenth-century England. That is, she was sheltered from knowing about 'the facts of life', especially about sex. This is her first time away from home, and it is her first job. At the beginning, she is, as she admits, naïve, innocent, and a bit frightened at the great responsibility facing her. She is unsophisticated and easily impressed with the house, with her employer, with the children.

She undertakes her duties enthusiastically and conscientiously. She is warm and loving towards the children, and she immediately gains their affection and that of Mrs Grose. Mrs Grose's respect for her indicates that she is capable and efficient in her work. When the ghosts begin to appear, she struggles to keep her self-control and to understand what is going on around her. She carefully thinks over every new circumstance and examines her own reactions to it. For the most part, her interpretations are subtle, sensitive and intelligent. She is courageous, and in spite of her inexperience, she can be firm and decisive when the time comes to act.

She does have some faults, mostly connected with her youth and her naïvety. She is overly romantic; she immediately falls in love with her employer, who has no interest in her, and she turns him, and everything associated with him—his house, the children—into objects of romantic regard. She tends to dramatise herself and her situation; from the beginning, she thinks of herself as a heroine in a novel. By her own admission, she is imaginative; she tends to have 'flights of fancy', to jump to conclusions, to give ordinary occurrences exciting and dramatic meaning. In forming judgements, she sometimes relies too heavily on her intuition, on her feelings about things, rather than on her reason. When the ghosts appear, she immediately 'senses' that they are there for the children, and jumps to the conclusion that the children must be saved from them. Her youthful vanity and pride lead her to think that she is the one who can save them; thus she can achieve her dreams of heroic achievement and attract their uncle's attention.

On an abstract level, the governess can be seen to represent youthful ignorance confronted by evil. She is among the many of James's heroes and heroines who undergo an 'initiation' into life through experience with it. She matures and becomes an adult when she learns about evil and confronts it in the form of the ghosts. Douglas's praise of her in the Prologue tells us that this experience has had a beneficial effect.

But it is dangerous to oversimplify our interpretation. The governess is a complex character, and the evil she confronts is subtle and ambiguous.

The children

We view the children, Miles and Flora, through the eyes of the governess. As the story progresses, their character undergoes a change. At first, to the governess, they are goodness and innocence itself; they have never known evil or unhappiness. They are perfectly beautiful, charming, and remarkably intelligent. They give the appearance, at least, of openness and frankness.

Yet the governess soon becomes aware that this goodness hides a kind of corruption, the exact nature of which is not clear. They *have* known evil, through their involvement with Peter Quint and Miss Jessel. They have, in fact, been encouraged in wrongdoing by their former servants, so that by the time the governess arrives at Bly, they have become accomplished little liars, playing a sinister game under a pretence of purity and innocence. However, Miles, who is more carefully portrayed than Flora, shows some signs of a genuine affection for the governess and a desire to resist the evil influence of the ghosts.

As the governess portrays them, they represent childish innocence, victimised and corrupted by an evil from which they can and must be saved.

Mrs Grose

Mrs Grose, the housekeeper, has several functions in the tale, although her character is simple and does not develop as the tale progresses. First, she is a source of information both for the governess and for the reader. Through her, certain significant points regarding the ghosts and the children can be introduced into the tale. In fact, she identifies the ghosts and tells the governess about their history and their corruption of the children.

Second, Mrs Grose is a 'foil' to the governess; that is, she is the opposite of the governess in character; and the contrast sets off and clarifies our picture of the governess. She is a good, simple, motherly woman, who adores the children and refuses to see any 'badness' in them. Although she is merely a servant and cannot read or write, she is a source of strength to the governess, who relies on her support and approval. In contrast to the governess, who continually tries to see the deeper meaning behind things, Mrs Grose accepts things as they appear to be. Thus, she cannot *see* evil, as the governess can, in the form of the ghosts. She represents solid, homey goodness and virtue, uncorrupting and uncorruptible.

Thus, finally, she is a practical person, whose good sense and truthfulness helps us to accept the wild speculations of the governess. *She* is reliable, we feel, and her confidence in the governess causes us to believe and trust her too. Her presence in the tale gives it an air of truth in spite of the strange occurrences. If she believes, then so can we.

The ghosts

There are two ghosts, each of which appears four times in the tale: Peter Quint, the uncle's former valet, and Miss Jessel, the children's former governess. In life, Quint was a 'hound', a 'devil'. But he was a handsome man who could bend women to his will. He seduced Miss Jessel, although he was a mere servant. She was a 'lady', both in her higher social position and in her morals and manners—at least until Quint came along. Quint's physical appearance is somewhat devilish; he has red hair, dark, arched eyebrows and burning eyes. Miss Jessel is a 'tragic figure' of 'unutterable woe'. Both died in mysterious circumstances, though separately. There is a hint that Quint's 'accidental' death may have been murder. Miss Jessel surely left Bly, as Mrs Grose suggests, because she was pregnant, and her death may have resulted from this, or, we are left to suppose, something worse, perhaps suicide or murder.

They have returned to 'reclaim' the children. As usual, James leaves ambiguities. Are the ghosts bent on further corruption of the children or do they want more—to draw the children with them into death? The evil associated with them seems to be primarily sexual in nature, though, again, this is not clear. Their sexual relationship would naturally have seemed particularly horrifying to an innocent parson's daughter, as well as to the moralistic Mrs Grose.

They represent the knowledge of worldly evil. For it is through them that the children learn to be 'bad', and through them that the governess learns about evil. They are the devils who enter the paradise of Bly, so that by the end of the tale, it has become a wintry world of corruption and death.

The uncle

The children's uncle, and their guardian, plays a minor but significant role in the story. He is handsome, dashing and romantic. He immediately captures the heart of the poor governess, though she sees him only twice. His role in the story is most significant in his influence on her; for her feelings for him influence her every action. For example, he charms her into accepting the job at Bly, and her fear of his annoyance prevents her from reporting Miles's dismissal from school.

He and Quint can be taken as foils. A parallel between them is suggested when the governess first sees Quint on the tower and momentarily mistakes him for her employer. Both are handsome and have an easy and compelling power over women. But *he* is a gentleman, and Quint is 'low'—at least in the governess's opinion. Viewing him as objectively as we can, we might think that he is probably a selfish, self-indulgent person, who cares little for the children. He desires to have nothing to do with them. Thus, in spite of what the governess wants to believe, he is clearly partly responsible for the corruption of the children.

But she idealises him as a kind of fairy-tale prince, whose love must be won through selfless and devoted service. Thus, he functions in the story in two ways; first, he serves as a romantic and idealised foil to set off the wickedness of Quint. Second, he provides a motive for much of what the governess does or does not do.

Douglas

Douglas is an interesting figure, although he appears only in the Prologue. He functions as the storyteller who makes the link between the real and the fantastic. He is a respectable figure whose testimony gives support to the governess's story. He is about sixty years old when he tells the story. He is somewhat romantic; for, after forty years, he is still in love with the governess. Thus he has a personal involvement in her story. There is a parallel between his relation to the governess and Miles's relation to her; that is, she was governess to Miles's sister and to Douglas's sister; she was ten years older than Miles when the events occurred and ten years older than Douglas when she told him about them. Moreover, his love for the governess represents one of the first ironic 'turns' in the story, for she is in love with someone else, the children's uncle. We might wonder if his love could influence his objectivity and cause him to give the governess higher praise than she deserves.

The narrator

The narrator, the unidentified 'I' who tells the tale, is often forgotten or overlooked by the reader, and with reason; for he seems to have no personality at all, except that he is interested in a good story and in the psychology and motives of others—a characteristic of James himself. That is, his function is to be the 'author' of the tale; he adds further distance between the reader and the story, while giving it an 'air of reality' because he too is presented as an objectively real person.

The problem

The complexity and ambiguity of *The Turn of the Screw* has puzzled many readers. Though seemingly simple, the story suggests a number of possible interpretations. A great deal about the characters, plot, and meaning is left unclear. A reader senses that there is something deeper to the tale than appears on the surface. The question arises: what is the 'deeper meaning' of this story, if, indeed, there is one? A number of critics who have studied this tale have suggested answers to this question. The most important of these is known as the 'hallucination theory' or the psychological theory. Other interpretations are mainly attempts to oppose the psychological theory or to reconcile it with a more traditional analysis of *The Turn of the Screw* as a simple ghost story.

The 'hallucination theory'

Hallucination refers to the seeing of objects that are not there. The hallucination theory focuses on the character of the governess. Even within a few years after the publication of *The Turn of the Screw* in 1898, a few readers began to question the truthfulness of her account and the wisdom of her behaviour. In the 1930s popular interest in psychology increased, mainly as a result of the writings of Sigmund Freud. Under the influence of Freudian ideas about the unconscious, about sexual repression, and about female hysteria, readers began to take a new look at *The Turn of the Screw*.

They observed that the entire tale is told by the governess; the reader perceives everything as she experiences it and as she understands it. He has no way of knowing if she is telling the truth. Some readers have concluded that she is not. They believe that the ghosts are not real, that the governess simply imagines them. Some suggest that she is emotionally disturbed, a neurotic, who does not distinguish between reality and her own imaginings. This view is known as the 'hallucination theory' because it argues that the ghosts are merely visions or hallucinations of the governess.

A good deal of internal evidence, from the story itself, can be put forward to support this view. The governess's descriptions of herself suggest that she is the kind of person likely to imagine ghosts. She is naïve, young, nervous, easily excitable. She is imaginative and tends to dramatise herself. She stays up late at night reading old novels and begins to think of herself as a heroine in a storybook.

She may have unconscious reasons for wanting to see the ghosts, reasons of which she is not fully aware. She is hopelessly in love with her employer, who is far above her in social class. When she first sees the ghost of Quint, she has been thinking about her employer. Her natural desire for romance expresses itself in this vision of a man on the tower, and later, of Miss Jessel. Miss Jessel was, like her, a governess to Miles and Flora; Quint is like the uncle in that he is attractive to women and dresses in the uncle's clothes. According to the hallucination theory, she expresses her repressed sexual feelings for her employer through the visions of these two lovers. Because her strict upbringing has taught her to regard these feelings as evil, she regards the relationship of Quint and Jessel as evil. Of course, all these feelings are unconscious, and she cannot express them openly.

In Chapter Six, however, she does admit that the ghosts provide her with a chance to be heroic and to attract the children's uncle.

> I now saw that I had been asked for a service admirable and difficult; and there would be a greatness in letting it be seen—oh, in the right quarter!—that I could succeed . . .

She refuses to contact the children's uncle or to send the children away from Bly, for this would look like failure on her part.

Moreover, the governess is unsure of herself. She continually questions her own perceptions and the conclusions she has drawn from them. She occasionally expresses doubts about her own sanity. For example, in Chapter Twenty, she is joyful when Miss Jessel appears on the lake because she thinks the appearance will prove that she was 'neither cruel nor mad'. She is so unsure of her suspicions about the children that she welcomes Miles's stealing because it 'justifies' them. Even in the final chapter, she has the 'appalling alarm' that Miles may be innocent. And she asks herself, '". . . if he *were* innocent, what then on earth was *I*?"'

Finally, the main evidence against the governess is that she is the *only* person to see the ghosts. Mrs Grose does not see them. We have only the governess's word that the children see them; and, as she admits, this is based on her 'intuition' and 'feeling' about the children and not on anything they say or do.

In fact, according to the hallucination theory, the children are innocent. Their behaviour does not support the governess's terrible accusations. Their little lies or 'bad' language can easily be explained as normal childish naughtiness. The only evidence of any kind that one of the children, Miles, sees the ghosts occurs in the final chapter, when he calls out, 'Peter Quint—you devil!' But by this time, he has had ample opportunity to guess what the governess wants him to say. His response can be seen as a pitiful, childish attempt to please her, so that she will cease her harassment of him. According to this view it is the governess who drives the children to hysteria and death by her constant pressure; it is she, rather than the ghosts, who 'turns the screw' like a torturer until she destroys them.

James himself provides some support for the 'hallucination theory'. In his preface to the New York Edition, he noted that one problem in writing the tale was to keep clear the governess's record of ambiguities and obscurities, by which, he says, 'I don't of course mean her explanation of them, a different matter.' That is, he seems to suggest that her understanding of what she sees may be mistaken. In this case, her mistake may extend so far that she does not realise her own unbalanced condition that leads her to see figures that are simply not there. Some critics argue that this was the trick 'to catch those not easily caught', mentioned by James in his preface. By drawing him into the mind of this neurotic young lady, James has duped the reader into accepting her story. After further thought, the reader may discover that he has been misled—a final 'turn of the screw' of irony.

No matter what James intended, many readers feel that the story is more relevant for them as a psychological study than as a ghost story. For most modern readers no longer believe in ghosts. They no longer think of evil as an independent force in the universe. To the modern reader, evil has its existence primarily in the mind of man. In their view, the 'deeper meaning' of the tale lies in the horror we feel as we watch this hysterical young woman, whose obsession leads her to destroy innocent children in the hope of 'saving' them from ghostly creations of her own tormented mind.

The traditional view

The hallucination theory has not been accepted by all readers. Much argument has been put forward to oppose it. According to the 'traditional' or 'orthodox' view of the story, there is no 'hidden meaning'. The story is clear as it is written: the governess is innocent; the ghosts are evil; the children are corrupt. In this view, the governess is a perfectly reliable narrator; her perceptions and conclusions must be taken as correct; and her efforts to save the children are indeed heroic.

Evidence in the story supports this view as well. The ghosts must be real, because in Chapter Five, the governess accurately describes Peter Quint to Mrs Grose although she has never seen or heard of him before. This point is very difficult to refute. (Some have made an effort to refute it by pointing out that in Chapter Five the governess indicates that, in spite of what she says, she does know something about the mysterious figure—she has found out that he is not someone from the village. This suggests that she has made inquiries and may know more than she admits.) Moreover, in the preface, James says that he has made the governess's story 'credible'; he has given her 'authority'. He does this through the testimony of the other characters. Douglas's love and respect for the governess testifies to the worth of her character. Douglas never suggests that she might have been hysterical or obsessed. The plain, practical Mrs Grose respects the governess and believes in her. The governess's self-doubts are natural under the circumstances.

Furthermore, those readers who prefer to see the story as a simple ghostly tale argue that if James had intended a psychological meaning, he would have made his intentions clear, both in the story and in his comments on it. They believe that modern critics are simply reading into the tale their own 'scientific' prejudices, and are thus reducing a thrilling and terrifying story to a mere psychological case study.

They too find support in James's own comments. In a letter to H.G. Wells of 9 December 1898, James indicates that he was more interested in the children than he was in the governess. She is there to tell about them; therefore, he had 'to rule out subjective complications of her own' and 'to keep her impersonal'. That is, he wants the reader to take her report as wholly objective; the reader should not become involved in questions about her personal psychology.

However, this is not to say that the traditional view rules out all psychological analysis of the governess. According to the traditionalists, the tale is not a case study of a neurotic; but it does provide insight into the mind of a sensitive, intelligent, and reliable young woman placed in a strange and dangerous situation. It is the study of the reactions of a normal, or above normal, young lady to the appearance of ghosts. Moreover, the traditionalists do not necessarily argue that the governess is always correct in her interpretations and responses. They believe, however, that her errors are caused by innocence and inexperience rather than by an hysterical obsession.

The difference between the two interpretations can be summed up in this question: Where does the evil lie? According to the traditional view, it is a real evil, active in the universe, and objectified and embodied in ghosts. According to the hallucination theory, the only evil in the story is that which exists in the governess's distorted and twisted mind. It is left to the reader to decide for himself.

Other interpretations

Two interpretations provide a compromise between the traditional view and the hallucination theory. The first of these has been suggested above: that James was fully aware of both possible interpretations and deliberately left the point unclear. According to this view, the theme of the story is the ambiguity of experience, the impossibility of ever being sure of our perceptions and interpretations. Like the governess, we can never be sure that our judgements are valid or that our actions are wise. This ambiguity is, in itself, a kind of evil that all of us have to learn to accept.

Thus the question of what really happens becomes irrelevant; the author does not really want us to know. Rather, like the governess, the reader is constantly called upon to revise his opinions, to reject his commonsense view of things, to adjust to new and strange circumstances. He may never reach a state of certainty, and this is the final irony, the final 'turn of the screw' for him; as the tale closes, instead of explanations, he finds himself left with questions and doubts.

Another view, very similar to the above, is that the story has several levels of meaning. That is, a reader can accept various interpretations at one time: it is both a simple ghost story and a psychological study of the governess. On one level, we can read it as a battle of her innocence against the forces of darkness; on another level, we can see it as a psychological study that locates the forces of darkness in the human mind. According to this view, James means to show that there are many explanations of life, of men and their motives and actions, of the nature of good and evil—all of them at least partly true.

The theme

The theme of the tale is the central idea. It should be a typical human experience, a view of life, that has universal application, that is valid for all men. In *The Turn of the Screw* the theme is not directly stated as a moral or a lesson for the reader. Instead, it is revealed through plot, characterisation, setting, atmosphere and style.

Each of the interpretations discussed above suggests a somewhat different theme, or central idea, for the story. The hallucination theory suggests that the meaning of the story is the development of an unconscious obsession in the mind of one person and the effects of this obsession on her and on those around her. According to this view, James was a brilliant psychologist who understood, even before Freud, the dangers of repressed love and the existence of the unconscious. For the most part, the governess is completely unaware of her true and hidden reasons for her actions. The reader learns that evil lies in the minds of men, in their tendency to distort reality to suit their own selfish interests and desires.

The traditional interpretation suggests that the theme of the story is that of innocence confronting evil, the 'initiation' theme. The young governess leaves her home for the first time and confronts life. She is initiated, introduced, into adulthood by her first experience with evil and danger. It is a test of her courage and character, and she proves herself equal to it. In this view, evil is not simply a 'twist' in the mind; it is a reality in the universe, which can, however, be overcome by courage and love.

A third interpretation argues that James was deliberately ambiguous, that any or all interpretations are valid. For to some readers, the theme of the tale *is* the ambiguity of experience which can be interpreted in many ways, none of them certain. According to their view, the theme of the tale lies in the method of its telling—in the use of the first-person narrator whose understanding is limited; in the progress of the tale by a series of ironic 'turns'; in the atmosphere of undefinable evil; and in the complexity and indirectness of the style.

Three points are common to all these interpretations, and these can be taken as constituting the theme of *The Turn of the Screw*. First, the tale is about innocence confronting evil. In the hallucination theory, the innocent children must battle against the evil in the mind of the governess. In the traditional view, the innocent governess confronts evil in the ghosts and in the corrupt children. Second, the story is about the deceptiveness of appearances. In the traditional view, the governess is deceived by the apparent pleasantness and beauty of Bly and the seeming innocence of the children. In the hallucination theory, the reader is deceived by the seeming innocence and good intentions of the governess.

Third, the story is about the ambiguity of experience. No matter what interpretation we accept, we must admit that James deliberately left many significant points unexplained—the evil nature of the ghosts, for example, or the extent of the children's involvement with them. The reader must interpret these for himself, but he can never be sure that his interpretations are wholly correct. Truth is relative, and each mind creates its own reality. According to the hallucination theory, the governess lives in a strange and sinister world of her own creation, a world which is in conflict with the experience of those around her. In the traditional view, the clarity and strength of mind of the governess allows her to penetrate through the deceit and wickedness of those around her, but only partly; her perceptions allow her only a 'sense' of evil, never a full understanding.

According to the third, and most inclusive view of the tale, the reader becomes aware that many interpretations are possible. Like life itself, the story is ambiguous; each reader must find his own truth in it, his own concept of good and evil. It is truly, as James said in the preface, a world 'in which nothing is right save as we rightly imagine it'.

In summary, three points stand out as significant to the meaning or theme of the tale: the confrontation of innocence with evil, the deceptiveness of appearances, and the ambiguity of experience.

Part 4

Hints for study

THIS PART is divided into three sections. The first, 'Points for study', suggests some topics and questions to keep in mind while studying the text of *The Turn of the Screw*. The second section, 'Suggestions for writing', gives general advice on how to develop and organise answers to examination questions about the story. The third section provides some sample discussion questions with model answers.

Points for study

As you read the tale, you should give attention to the following topics and questions:

The theme or meaning of the tale. What typical human experience does it depict? How is this theme revealed in the characters and the plot? Is it related to other elements of the tale—setting, atmosphere, point of view, style? Does it contribute to the effect of the tale? Does the author state it directly?

NOTE: In answering questions about the theme, it is best to be as clear and simple as possible; adopt one interpretation and stick to it.

The setting. What is the setting? Does it contribute to the effect of the tale? Does it have any other special functions? Does the setting change as the story progresses? Does this change reflect any development in the characters or plot?

The characters.

The governess. What kind of person is she? Does her character change during the story? What are the motives that influence her behaviour? To what degree is she aware of these motives?

The children, Flora and Miles. Are they innocent or corrupt? Does their character change as the story progresses? How does the reader's view of their character compare with that of the governess?

The ghosts, Peter Quint and Miss Jessel. What is their function in the tale? Under what circumstances do they appear? What is the nature of the evil they represent?

The minor figures. What is their function? Do they provide motives for the actions of the major characters? Do they provide information about, or comments on, the action or the major characters? Consider: Mrs Grose, Douglas, the children's uncle, the unidentified narrator.

The Prologue. What is the function of the Prologue? Does it help the reader to accept the story? Why does the tale end suddenly without a return to the situation of the Prologue?

The point of view. Why is the story told in the first person? Is it significant that the narrator also participates in the story? Is the narrator honest? Can we trust her report? Is the point of view important to the theme of the story?

The atmosphere. What feeling is aroused in the reader? How does the author achieve this atmosphere? How does he achieve suspense? What is the total effect of the story on the reader? Is this effect related to the theme?

The style. What are some characteristics of James's style of writing? What meaning or effect is conveyed in his style? Why is the tale so ambiguous? Does the ambiguity have any relation to the theme of the tale?

The structure of the tale. What is the climax of the tale? How does the author build up to this climax? Does the construction of the tale follow any kind of pattern?

The conflict in the tale, the plot. What is the nature of the conflict in the tale? Between whom does it occur? In what way is it resolved? Is this resolution satisfactory in terms of the story itself, of the theme, or of the reader's expectations?

The function of individual episodes. Which episodes stand out most clearly in the mind of a reader? Do these episodes represent key points in the story or 'turns' in the action? In what way do they reveal character? In what way do they advance the plot?

The title. Is the title mentioned in the tale? Does it refer to the structure of the tale? Does it suggest the meaning of the tale?

Suggestions for writing

Remember that good writing is clear, concise and well organised. As you write, keep the following suggestions in mind:

Begin with a clear topic sentence. The topic sentence should restate the question and it should indicate the major points which will be developed in your answer. For example, if the question is, 'What is the function of Mrs Grose in the story?' you might begin by saying: 'Mrs Grose has three important functions in *The Turn of the Screw*: She provides information about the children and the ghosts; she serves as a foil to the governess; and she contributes an air of reality to the tale.'

Organise your answer. Develop each point in one paragraph. Arrange your points in some logical order, such as cause and effect, or order of importance.

Support your major points with relevant evidence from the text. Refer to specific conversations or scenes. Include appropriate quotations if possible. Show your reader that you are familiar with the tale.

Write simply and clearly. Avoid long sentences. Make clear connections between ideas. Do not depend on your reader to guess what you mean; be direct and precise.

Answer the question. Note the directions carefully and follow them exactly. If you are directed to tell *why* something happened, then tell *why*, not *how*. Do not answer a specific question with a summary of the story, unless such a summary is called for in the question.

Stick to the subject. Do not make statements or include unnecessary details that are irrelevant to the question. Do not try to tell the reader everything that you know about the story.

Be selective. Because *The Turn of the Screw* is ambiguous in meaning, the answer to almost any question about it will involve an element of interpretation. Do not try to cover all the possible interpretations. Decide on one interpretation, stick to it, and support it with evidence from the story.

Stick closely to the tale itself. Draw on it for your arguments and your evidence. Avoid generalisations about the personality of the author, about the nature of the short story, or about anything else external to the tale itself, unless you know the subject well or unless such information is called for in the question.

Sample questions

Below are a number of sample questions about *The Turn of the Screw*. Answers are provided as models for your own writing.

Question 1: Is the governess a reliable narrator?

SAMPLE ANSWER:
Although some readers believe that the governess in *The Turn of the Screw* is an unreliable narrator whose testimony cannot be trusted, evidence in the story indicates that Henry James intended the reader to accept her story as true and her interpretations as correct. In the first place, the other characters in the tale respect her and have confidence in her. In the Prologue, Douglas testifies to the high quality of her

character: 'She was a most charming person . . . She was the most agreeable woman I've ever known in her position; she would have been worthy of any whatever.' There is no doubt that he believes her story. Moreover, her employer, the children's uncle, trusts her so much that he gives her full charge of the children. Like him, Mrs Grose has an immediate feeling of confidence in the governess. And she maintains this confidence throughout most of the story in spite of the fact that she cannot see the ghosts. At no point in the story does any other character question the honesty or reliability of the governess.

In the second place, details in the story show clearly that the governess really does see the ghosts and that her suspicions about the children are correct. We know that the governess sees the ghosts because of her descriptions of them to Mrs Grose. For example, in Chapter Eight, she gives a clear and detailed description of Peter Quint, even though she has never seen him before. Furthermore, objective evidence in the story supports her suspicions that the children are corrupt. Miles has been dismissed from school because he is 'an injury to the others'. Mrs Grose tells the governess that the children were under the influence of the wicked Quint and Jessel and knew about their immoral behaviour. Miles lied about his relationship with Peter Quint. Other evidence is provided by their strange wanderings at night, which they cannot explain adequately.

In the last few chapters of the story, the governess's suspicions are confirmed. Flora uses some of the filthy language that she learned from Quint and Jessel. Miles steals a letter; and he confesses that he 'said things' at school which were, indeed, bad. Finally, in the last chapter, Miles shows clearly that he has known about the ghosts. He names Miss Jessel to the governess, although she has never mentioned Miss Jessel to him. And he calls out to the ghost that he can no longer see: 'Peter Quint—you devil!'

Thus, the testimony of other characters and the details of the story indicate that James meant us to accept the governess as a reliable narrator.

Question 2: Is Miles's death at the end of the story justified?

SAMPLE ANSWER :
Miles's sudden death at the end of the story can be justified for two reasons. In the first place, it is necessary to the effect of the story. Secondly, it results naturally from events in the story itself.

Miles's death is one of the means by which James achieves the 'uncanny' horror promised the reader in the Prologue. The sense of approaching disaster gradually builds up throughout the tale, as the governess becomes aware of the ghostly danger to the children. Her fears are finally realised with Miles's death. The effect on the reader is one of dismay and horror. Any happier ending, such as the defeat of the ghosts by the governess, might suggest that the danger had not been so great after all. The reader would be left with a feeling of pleasure rather than of horror and shock. Miles's death is a testimony to the reality of the evil that has threatened him throughout the tale.

Second, Miles's death occurs naturally and inevitably as the result of the events in the story. He has become 'possessed' by a demon, the ghost of Quint. The governess continually remarks that the children act under the influence of the ghosts. When Miles dies, the governess says that his heart has stopped because it has been 'dispossessed'. His being 'possessed' means that the ghost has entered into him, taken him over, and become part of his very life. Thus, when he is finally cut off from Quint, part of himself is destroyed, and he cannot survive.

Another reason for Miles's death also grows out of the conflict in the story. The governess tells us, '. . . the strain had been too much'. Miles has been torn between his loyalty to the governess and his attraction to Quint. The torment of being torn between two loyalties is so great that the young boy is physically unable to stand the strain, and he dies. We are prepared for his death when the governess, clutching him, feels 'the tremendous pulse of his little heart': His death reveals how truly great was the hold of the ghost over him, and yet, in contrast, how great was his desire to be free of it. His death is the ultimate horror of the tale, the final 'turn of the screw' for the governess and the reader.

Question 3: What is the function of the Prologue of the tale?

SAMPLE ANSWER:
The Prologue of James's *The Turn of the Screw* serves three major functions. First, it establishes the atmosphere of the tale. Second, it gives the tale credibility by setting it in a frame. Third, it provides information necessary to an understanding of the tale which could not easily be provided in the governess's own account.

First, the Prologue draws the reader gradually into the tale by introducing him to a group of friends who are telling ghost stories around a fire one December night. They have already heard one tale and are prepared by Douglas for another which is even more 'gruesome'. Thus, James immediately establishes the atmosphere of mystery, terror, and suspense, which he develops as the story progresses. The setting by the fire, the wintry darkness outside, creates an atmosphere of the uncanny, the strange, and a sense of being cut off from the everyday world. Because of it, the reader is able to suspend his disbelief and to accept the events he is about to hear.

Second, the Prologue also gives the tale credibility. The tale is introduced by two narrators, who are presented as 'real' people. But one of them, Douglas, has known the governess to whom the events occurred. As we learn about the governess from Douglas, who passionately believes in her, we come to accept his faith that what she has written down is wholly true. Douglas gives the story credibility because he believes in it and because he has confidence in the governess, whose story it is.

The Prologue not only establishes the atmosphere of the story and gives it credibility, it also allows the author to give the reader a good deal of information about the heroine of the tale. This information could not easily have been included in the governess's manuscript. Yet much of it is essential to a full understanding of the tale. Through Douglas, we learn of the governess's family background and of the circumstances that lead her to take the work at Bly. We learn of her naïvety and lack of sophistication, which causes her to fall immediately in love with her employer. This love suggests her romantic nature. We find out that this is her first employment and that she is extremely nervous about it, though she is encouraged by her sense of duty and devotion to her employer. That is, through Douglas, we have a fairly good understanding of the governess's character before we begin reading her tale.

Question 4: What is the advantage of having the story told in the first person by a narrator who participates in the action?

SAMPLE ANSWER:

In *The Turn of the Screw* Henry James makes use of the device of the first person narrator—a governess who tells her own story in her own words. There are several good reasons why he chose this method of narration. In the first place, it gives the tale an air of reality. The reader is disposed to believe the story because it is presented as a true account involving a person who really lived.

Second, the use of a narrator allows the events to be presented from a single, limited point of view. This point of view contributes to the suspense and to the effect of the tale. The reader does not confront an all-knowing author, who should be able to tell him everything but who refuses to, do so. Instead, the reader knows only what the governess knows, and he understands only what she understands. Thus, the author builds up suspense by leaving the reader in doubt as to what will happen next. The reader is slowly drawn into the events along with the governess; he shares her puzzlement and confusion. He finds himself, like her, trying to find a reasonable explanation for the ghosts. And failing, he comes to share her sense of danger and horror. Her limited responses direct and limit the responses of the reader and allow the author to achieve a concentrated and intense effect.

Finally, James uses the first person narrator to change the tale from simply another ghost story into the study of human psychology. The tale is not only about the ghosts and their danger to the children; it is also about one person's reactions to this danger. The ghosts and the children are interesting because of the effect they produce on the governess. The reader is able to examine this effect directly, because he follows the workings of her mind. And he comes to understand characteristics of her personality which she herself may not be aware of. He sees how her naïvety, her tendency to romanticise herself, and her vanity determine her responses to the ghosts.

In summary, the first person narrator gives credibility to the story. Moreover, the first person point of view creates suspense by limiting the knowledge of the reader to that of one character; it draws the reader into the story and makes him feel as if he is also a participant in it; and thus it increases his growing sense of horror. Finally, the first person narrator allows the author to expand his tale so that it is not just another ghost story but a study of human psychology.

Question 5: What is the theme of *The Turn of the Screw*?

SAMPLE ANSWER:
The theme of Henry James's *The Turn of the Screw* is the confrontation of innocence with evil for the first time. The governess is innocence itself. Brought up in a strict and unsophisticated home, she is introduced to evil, for the first time in her life, in the form of the ghosts of Quint and Jessel. She fights against this evil which threatens the innocent children, Miles and Flora. The nature of this evil is unclear, but it does include sexual wrongdoing, as represented by the illicit relationship of Quint and Jessel. This relationship is associated, moreover, with lies, deceit, trickery, and with the desire of the ghosts to dominate and destroy the children. This is the governess's first acquaintance with such qualities.

Furthermore, through the ghosts and their effect on the children, the governess learns that evil is secret, indirect, and ambiguous. She discovers that it may be concealed behind the sweetest faces and the most charming behaviour. She learns that evil does not operate openly, but through lies and treachery; the ghosts work behind her back to corrupt the children; the children kiss her and play with her in order to prevent her suspicions. Evil, she discovers, is not easily detected or understood. It reveals itself in the children as an attitude—a growing love of deceit and wrongdoing for its own sake—rather than an action that can be seen and dealt with directly. For the secret corruption of the children is not clearly revealed in their behaviour; rather their behaviour is a 'pretence', a 'fraud' behind which they conceal the 'knowledge of all evil'.

Thus, *The Turn of the Screw* is about a young woman's first knowledge of evil and her growing understanding of it. The governess, at the beginning of the tale, is a naïve and romantic young girl. By the end, she has become aware of all the possibilities of evil as it operates through human nature. And she comes to accept it as an inevitable part of life. When the ghosts first appear, when she first learns about Quint and Jessel from Mrs Grose, she is dismayed and horrified. But as the tale progresses, she gradually loses her fear. By Chapter Sixteen she is relaxed enough to refer to Miss Jessel jokingly as her 'visitor'. By Chapter Twenty-two, she has reached a full understanding that evil is a reality that she must accept and try to deal with; she can no longer deny it or pretend that it does not exist. It is part of human nature, another 'turn of the screw of ordinary human virtue'.

Part 5

Suggestions for further reading

The text

The text is readily available in the Penguin Modern Classics Edition, Penguin Books, Harmondsworth.

The Uniform Tales of Henry James, Martin Secker, London, 1915, contains the revisions James made for the New York edition of his *Works*, Charles Scribner's Sons, New York, 1908; and Macmillan, London, 1908.

General reading

About Henry James:

DUPEE, F.W.: *Henry James*, Delta Books, revised edition, New York, 1965.

EDEL, LEON: *Henry James* (University of Minnesota Pamphlets on American Writers, No. 4), University of Minnesota Press, Minneapolis, 1960. A brief introduction to Henry James designed for the beginning student.

EDEL, LEON: *The Life of Henry James*, Penguin Books, Harmondsworth, 1978. A two-volume paperback edition of the five-volume definitive biography by Leon Edel.

POWERS, LYALL H.: *Henry James: An Introduction and Interpretation*, Holt, Rinehart and Winston, New York, 1970.

About 'The Turn of the Screw'

CRANFILL, THOMAS M. AND ROBERT L. CLARK: *An Anatomy of 'The Turn of the Screw'*, University of Texas Press, Austin, Texas, 1965.

KIMBROUGH, ROBERT (ED.): *Henry James: The Turn of the Screw* (Norton Critical Editions), W.W. Norton, New York, 1966. A casebook, a collection of critical essays.

WEST, MURIEL: *A Stormy Night with 'The Turn of the Screw'*, Frye and Smith, Phoenix, Arizona, 1964.

WILLEN, GERALD (ED.): *A Casebook on Henry James's 'The Turn of the Screw'*, second edition, Thomas Y. Crowell, New York, 1969. A collection of critical essays.

The author of these notes

MARY HALLAB, a native of Louisiana, was educated at Louisiana State University where she obtained an MA and Ph.D in English. For the past ten years she has lived in the Middle East, and she is currently Assistant Professor of English at the American University of Beirut, Lebanon. She is a member of the editorial board of the *Review of English Studies in the Arab World*. At present, she is working on a handbook of English for Arab students, which is funded by the Ford Foundation, and a book on Henry James.

The first 100 titles

(* available Autumn 1980)

MRS GASKELL	*North and South*
WILLIAM GOLDING	*Lord of the Flies*
OLIVER GOLDSMITH	*The Vicar of Wakefield*
THOMAS HARDY	*Jude the Obscure*
	★ *Tess of the D'Urbervilles*
	★ *The Mayor of Casterbridge*
	The Return of the Native
	★ *The Trumpet Major*
L.P. HARTLEY	★ *The Go-Between*
ERNEST HEMINGWAY	★ *For Whom the Bell Tolls*
	The Old Man and the Sea
ANTHONY HOPE	★ *The Prisoner of Zenda*
RICHARD HUGHES	*A High Wind in Jamaica*
THOMAS HUGHES	*Tom Brown's Schooldays*
HENRIK IBSEN	★ *A Doll's House*
HENRY JAMES	★ *The Turn of the Screw*
BEN JONSON	★ *The Alchemist*
	Volpone
D.H. LAWRENCE	*Sons and Lovers*
	★ *The Rainbow*
HARPER LEE	★ *To Kill a Mocking-Bird*
SOMERSET MAUGHAM	*Selected Short Stories*
HERMAN MELVILLE	*Billy Budd*
	★ *Moby Dick*
ARTHUR MILLER	★ *Death of a Salesman*
	The Crucible
JOHN MILTON	★ *Paradise Lost I & II*
SEAN O'CASEY	*Juno and the Paycock*
GEORGE ORWELL	*Animal Farm*
	★ *Nineteen Eighty-four*
JOHN OSBORNE	★ *Look Back in Anger*
HAROLD PINTER	★ *The Birthday Party*
J.D. SALINGER	*The Catcher in the Rye*

SIR WALTER SCOTT	*Ivanhoe* *Quentin Durward*
WILLIAM SHAKESPEARE	*A Midsummer Night's Dream* *Antony and Cleopatra* *Coriolanus* *Cymbeline* *Hamlet* *Henry IV Part I* *Henry V* *Julius Caesar* *King Lear* *Macbeth* *Much Ado About Nothing* *Othello* *Richard II* *Romeo and Juliet* *The Merchant of Venice* *The Tempest* *The Winter's Tale* *Troilus and Cressida* *Twelfth Night*
GEORGE BERNARD SHAW	*Androcles and the Lion* *Arms and the Man* *Caesar and Cleopatra* *Pygmalion*
RICHARD BRINSLEY SHERIDAN	*The School for Scandal*
JOHN STEINBECK	*Of Mice and Men* *The Grapes of Wrath* *The Pearl*
ROBERT LOUIS STEVENSON	*Kidnapped* *Treasure Island*
JONATHAN SWIFT	*Gulliver's Travels*
W.M. THACKERAY	*Vanity Fair*
MARK TWAIN	*Huckleberry Finn* *Tom Sawyer*
VOLTAIRE	*Candide*
H.G. WELLS	*The History of Mr Polly* *The Invisible Man* *The War of the Worlds*
OSCAR WILDE	*The Importance of Being Earnest*